NICARAGUA

The People Speak

NICARAGUA
The
People Speak

Alvin Levie

FOREWORD BY
Dr. Richard Streb

Bergin & Garvey Publishers, Inc.
MASSACHUSETTS

All photographs in this book were taken by the author.

First published in 1985 by Bergin & Garvey Publishers, Inc.
670 Amherst Road
South Hadley, Massachusetts 01075

56789   987654321

Printed in the United States of America

LIBRARY OF CONGRESS CATALOGING-IN-PUBLICATION DATA

Levie, Alvin.
  Nicaragua : the people speak.

  1. Nicaragua—Politics and government—1979–
2. Interviews—Nicaragua. I. Title.
F1528.L48   1985   972.85'05   85-13485
ISBN 0-89789-083-3
ISBN 0-89789-084-1 (pbk.)

Design by Stanley S. Drate/Folio Graphics Co. Inc.

*To all people everywhere
who are willing to fight
for their freedom and dignity.*

Acknowledgements

Many people, most of whom I'll never know, made this book possible. My thanks to them and to Melba Altimirando, Ann Levie, Emilio Rodriguez, Bill Secord, Rudy Simons, Dick Streb, Joan Uhlen, Orlando Watson, and above all, to Edith, for her unfailing support and encouragement.

Contents

Foreword

In all human history comparatively few people have participated in or lived through a social revolution. Fewer still have been able to journey to a land in the midst of revolution and observe and record the process. That, in fact, is the situation in Nicaragua today. More people from all over the globe have journeyed to Nicaragua to observe the process as it unfolds than in any previous revolution. Its openness is an outstanding characteristic of the Nicaraguan revolution.

It is essential for Americans at this time in our history to focus our attention on what is happening to the poor people of Nicaragua. We must ask what we can do and what we must not do. The answer lies in our history and in the history of the relationship between the United States and Nicaragua.

Let us look at Nicaragua. It is the largest country in Central America; about the size of Iowa or Michigan or North Carolina. Its population is approximately that of Iowa.

It is abundant with rich agricultural lands and enormous potential for geothermal and hydroelectric energy development. It has important timber resources and minerals, and it has great waterways. It is the outstanding location for an Atlantic-Pacific sea-level canal.

The question of a sea-level canal runs all through Nicaraguan and United States relations. Many treaties have been signed by the U.S. and Nicaragua at various times, all designed to give the United States the right to build and control that canal.

President Johnson appointed a commission to study the canal question in 1967. The results were published in 1970. There were many conclusions and recommendations. Two have direct bearing on U.S.-Nicaraguan relations: (1) The present Panama Canal (a lock canal) is already out of date. At any given moment there may be twenty or thirty vessels anchored on the Atlantic or Pacific side waiting their turn to pass through the locks. The largest vessels are too wide and cannot use the present canal. (2) Without a sea level canal, by the year 2,000, world trade will be seriously (adversely) affected. The Nicaraguan potential for the canal has not changed. We're just not talking about it.

During the U.S.-Mexican War, President Polk made a serious effort to win the right to build and control a canal through Nicaraguan territory. These maneuvers coincided and overlapped with the discovery of gold and the world-wide rush to California starting in 1849. The easiest routes to California from the U.S. East Coast and from Europe was by sea and then across the Isthmus of Panama, or across Nicaragua. With the help of the U.S. government, Commodore Vanderbilt got the right to organize and operate the Accessory Transit route through Nicaragua. By 1853 his company carried one-third of the thousands of gold-seekers rushing to California. The Accessory Transit Company was a combination coach and boat transportation. In three years this business made him $8 million. It also made him many enemies.

One result was a mob uprising in Greytown on the Nicaraguan Atlantic Coast. A consular official from the U.S. had his face bruised in the melee. In the absense of an apology from the leaders of the uprising, the U.S. naval commander ordered a bombardment which wiped the village off the map. U.S. marines were then sent ashore to demolish the two buildings that remained standing after the bombardment.

Again, during the period of political infighting between the Conservatives of Granada (pro British) and the Liberals of Leon (pro U.S.), when it appeared that the Liberals might lose control of the national government, the U.S. minister urged the Liberal leaders to hire William Walker with his 150 armed mercenaries, then waiting in San Francisco. Walker took charge and appointed himself President of Nicaragua in 1856. As President, he made English the official language, legalized slavery, invited foreign investment on most favorable terms, and schemed to conquer additional Central American countries.

Walker's interest clashed with Vanderbilt's, and eventually he lost the presidency and was driven from the country. Walker attempted to reconquer the land on two occasions. Eventually, the British captured him and turned him over to the Hondurans who promptly shot him. September 14 is Independence Day in Nicaragua—the day that the decisive battle against Walker was fought at San Jacinto.

Another example of the Nicaraguan reality—Nicaragua elected a progressive nationalist, Jose Zelaya, President in 1893. Zelaya worked hard to develop Nicaragua. He initiated a railroad building program, extended the road system substantially, improved port facilities, extended public education, created employment by starting a public works program.

To effectuate his reforms Zelaya had to gain control of the Atlantic Coast region (the first time in Nicaraguan history that this had been done). He collected customs and controlled the ports. The foreign companies operating in Nicaragua (lumber, mines, coffee, and bananas) were made to pay reasonable taxes and obey national laws. Subsequently, the U.S. denounced Zelaya as a dictator, and an anti-American disturber of the peace.

The U.S. turned to the Panama Canal route in part because with Zelaya in power we couldn't get "our" conditions and control to build a Nicaraguan canal. After the U.S. started construction of the Panama route, Zelaya negotiated with the Germans to build a second canal. The U.S. government then fomented a rebellion and used the execution of two mercenaries on Zelaya's order as an excuse to threaten intervention. Zelaya resigned his office to forestall further U.S. actions.

The U.S. government sent Thomas Dawson to reorganize Nicaraguan finances. Nicaragua was forced to accept a large loan and then the U.S. took over the customs collections to guarantee repayment of the loan. We reorganized the police and military, established a national bank and supervised it. A popular reaction to U.S. domination resulted in civil disturbances in 1912, and this lead to the U.S. marines landing in Bluefields on the Atlantic and Corinto on the Pacific.

One general resisted this U.S. occupation. He was Benjamin Zeledon, who was subsequently shot, and his body strapped to a horse and led through villages to terrorize any potential resisters into submission. Zelaya and Zeledon are Nicaraguan heroes.—this is a part of the Nicaraguan reality.

The U.S. marines remained in Nicaragua from 1912 to 1934 with one nine-month exception in 1925. During the 1920s United Fruit, Standard Fruit, and Braggman's Bluff Lumber Company and other U.S. corporations enjoyed an orgy of exploitation. Braggman's, for example, is responsible for much of the deforested area in the north-central highlands. More of the Nicaraguan reality.

In 1926-27, there was growing unrest and the U.S. marines were strengthened and proceeded to "kick butt." One man resisted. He was Augusto C. Sandino. For the next five years Sandino engaged our marines in a full scale war. In an attempt to put an end to his resistance, the marine air corps bombed civilians (the second such attack in history) in the town of Ocotal on July 17, 1927.

The successful resitance won world-wide attention. The U.S. was exposed as a bully and worse. A ragged, poorly equipped group of peasants—never more than 300—had held off the mighty United States. It was a costly affair, costly in U.S. lives and dollars, and after five years there was no end in sight, no light at the end of the tunnel.

Thus, a decision was made to train and equip a national guard to police Nicaragua so that we could withdraw our armed forces. Everything was in place by 1932 and Hoover proceeded to withdraw our marines in that year. Roosevelt completed the action in 1933. Anastasio Somoza was appointed head of the national guard. Thus began what was to become a forty-six year history of the Somoza family dictatorship—one of the cruelest, greediest, in history.

There is no record of any U.S. President expressing concern about democracy or freedom during this forty-six year period. There is no record of any President pressuring Somoza to moderate his tyrranical ways. As Franklin Roosevelt said, "He may be a son-of-a-bitch, but he is *our* son-of-a-bitch."

Somoza paid well for our support. He provided the land and cover to train Castillo Armas and his forces when he was engaged by the CIA to overthrow the elected government of Jacobo Arbenz in Guatemala in 1954. He offered to send troops to fight in Korea. His son and heir provided land to train and launch the CIA sponsored Bay of Pigs invasion of Cuba in 1961.

The Somozas were exceedingly kind to foreign corporations exploiting Nicaraguan national resources. For example, to produce gold in equivilent in value to $7 million or $8 million a year, 6,796 Nicaraguan employees received average wages of five cordobas (U.S. $0.65) for an eight-hour day under wretched conditions. The government took 3.5 percent of the profits, to which was added the 2.25 percent "additional contribution" pocketed by Somoza. By the time the elder Somoza was assassinated in 1956, Nicaragua was an extreme example of a dependent economy. The economy of this weak country was externally oriented and the government controlled by a national and international elite that benefitted from that control and dependency. The people of Nicaragua were considered a source of cheap labor—exploitable producers—not consumers.

All the markets for Nicaraguan products were external ones. Evermore land was given-over to commercial crops—coffee, sugar, tobacco, cotton. Less land was available for fruit and vegetable production for local consumption. The means of production and income therefrom was concentrated in very few hands. The gross national product grew—but it never "trickled down."

By the time of their downfall the Somoza family holdings were in excess of $1 and a half billion. It owned 23 percent of all arable land in the nation. The Somozas owned most of the food processing and packaging industry and all export-import franchises. They owned urban real estate, sea ports, the national maritime and air lines, construction and mining companies, banks, hotels, restaurants, houses of prostitution, the fishing industry, parking meters, auto dealerships and on and on and on.

The legacy of the U.S. protected Somoza dynasty, was for the people of Nicaragua, among the most wretched in the Western Hemisphere. Infant mortality, malnutrition, illiteracy, starvation, brutality, degredation, was a way of life for the majority of Nicaraguans.

The struggle to rid themselves of this tyrant was far more costly than the U.S. struggle to free ourselves of George III's grip: 50,000 lives lost, 100,000 wounded, 150,000 homeless, 40,000 orphaned, 1,000,000 unemployed, etc. More than $500 million physical damage to plants and equipment, $80 million in damages to housing, hospitals, transportation and commerce. The Sandinistas inherited a debt of almost $2 billion. Anastasio Somoza stole all but $300 million of the national reserves. This is a part of the Nicaraguan reality not generally known to citizens of the U.S..

As a member of a January, 1984, Witness for Peace delegation, Mr. Levie was among thousands making the journey to this land so intimately connected with our own.

A life-long activist, he listened carefully to representatives from youth, labor, law, education, women's groups, the press, government, religion, business, and the like. Later, reflecting on his experience, Mr. Levie realized that he had missed a very important element of this contemporary drama. He had compiled facts, figures, and historical data, but somehow the voice, the thoughts, the feelings, and problems of the *people* were missing. He needed to know the worker, peasant, artisan, mechanic, fisherman, professional, street vendor. He wanted to capture the voice of Nicaraguense—the voice of the people of Nicaragua. He wanted to capture the voice of a people in the midst of social change.

Movements—revolutions—says Levie, are made by people, "in all their wondrous variety." He believes that people act on their *perceptions* of reality—on their individual needs, histories, aspirations.

Further, according to the author, the history of our time is the drama of colonial, oppressed, people finding and fighting their way to freedom. To know the Nicaraguan people is to begin to know all "Third World" people, and the dynamic of modern history.

In pursuit of this goal Mr. Levie returned to Nicaragua and crossed the country from coast to coast, border to border. He lived in the homes of campesinos, fishermen, mechanics, washerwomen. He listened carefully to individuals from every walk of life. The result is this fascinating and valuable documentary. Fascinating, because it brings to life the people to be found in the underdeveloped world. We are reminded that not all people in Nicaragua—anymore than in the North American colonies of 1776—play roles in the revolutionary process. We are reminded that for the poor mere survival requires enormous effort and energy. For the "haves," change is neither needed nor wanted.

Mr. Levie's book makes clear the enormous complexity in human affairs even in this relatively simple society. The wide variety of political thought and sophistication, the social awareness or lack of it, the sense of commitment or failure to understand the need for it at this time in their history, the variety of life styles and values, the multiplicity of work processes and patterns and the drive for a better life and for peace. Therein lies the value of this book. The very complexity of the lives of Mr. Levie's subjects and their views should equip U.S. readers to avoid simplistic slogans, easy solutions, and demogogic appeals to national pride.

Hopefully, it will help us to better understand the world in which we live. Hopefully, it will help us, North Americans, to better understand our role and our responsibilities.

DR. RICHARD STREB
Teachers College
Columbia University

Preface

This book is a particle of history—as I saw it. It is a view of Nicaragua five years after the conclusion of the revolution in that land. The reality of contemporary Nicaragua is told in the words of its people.

In gathering material for this book during the spring and summer of 1984 I traveled throughout Nicaragua. I spent time and listened carefully to hundreds of Nicaraguans in thirteen of the nation's sixteen departments. I spoke with people of every social class and stratum—farmers, both large and small; industrial workers and their employers; merchants; businessmen; housewives; fishermen; students; laborers; the unemployed; and so on. Those whose statements are included I consider to be representative of many.

I deliberately avoided the leaders of the revolution—and counter-revolution. Instead, in the countryside I sought out the campesinos, the faceless ones we North Americans so often wave at from our fast-moving vehicles and then quickly forget. In the cities and towns I did much the same. I listened carefully to those whom we usually wonder about fleetingly, and then, equally quickly, permit to fade into anonymity. I visited the factories and the docks. On the Atlantic coast I sought out Miskitos in the bush, Blacks, Creoles, and the dominant Mestizos. I was rarely, if ever, disappointed in the Nicaraguan people's willingness to talk openly, frankly, without reservation.

I also deliberately avoided investigation or analysis of the "institutions" of "the process"[1] except to the extent that they influence the consciousness and thought processes of the people. Nicaragua's massive literacy, health, and other social programs have been amply documented elsewhere. The land distribution programs, child development centers, reeducation and rehabilitation programs are the subjects of many excellent studies and books. The nation's reforestation, industrialization, land reclamation, government, and military

---

[1]Sometimes referred to as "the revolutionary process." It refers to the ongoing structural and ideological changes in Nicaragua.

organization have all been well documented. Thus, for many, this book may stimulate more questions than it answers. For it deals exclusively with that most mysterious and elusive of subjects—people.

Not surprisingly, I found the Nicaraguan people to be breathtaking in their variety. Also not surprisingly, where politics and the direction of modern Nicaraguan history are concerned, the people tended to conform to given economic and social patterns. Yet even here I had many dramatic surprises.

What occurred in Nicaragua in July 1979 was not an election, a referendum, a traditional Latin American *golpe*.[2] In 1979, power—political and economic—was wrenched from one class by another after prolonged, bloody conflict. The large landowners, industrialists, merchants, and their allies lost. The long-suffering campesinos, wage workers, and their allies won. It was as simple as that.

Yet, for many, including even some who helped to bring about the Sandinista victory, this concept is difficult, if not impossible, to understand. For, something more was involved than the immediate transfer of wealth and political power. The Sandinista victory marked a break with national history. It heralded a qualitative change in social relationships, a new body of social values—an impossible pill for many to swallow.

A typical example is the Sandinista view of large landowners and industrialists as *stewards* of the nation's wealth rather than as entrepreneurs concerned solely with personal gain. Business people who produce, who contribute to the nation's wealth and well-being, are entitled to ample financial reward. But woe to whoever decapitalizes, allows good land to lie fallow, or otherwise diminishes the nation's wealth. That person may quickly and irrevocably forfeit the (people's) property in question.

What is involved is more than the simple transfer of power and riches. The Sandinistas, who claim that their ideology combines Marxist socialism with Christian values, know that well. For along with economic transformation they *must* also accomplish a transformation of social thought in order to survive. They *need to* develop and popularize an *ideology* in order to ensure the survival of the "New Nicaragua." The Nicaraguan people are engaged in a social revolution and counterrevolution. They must be ideologically armed to withstand the blows of their antagonists.

[2]Literally, 'a blow'; commonly used to denote coups, palace revolts, etc.

What of the people of Nicaragua? For in the final analysis it is they who will determine the success or demise of "the process." Who are they? What do they think? What have they gained—or lost—from the revolution? What are their aspirations? How deep is their commitment to change—or to a return to pre-Sandinista Nicaragua? Are sufficient numbers of them prepared to struggle, sacrifice, fight, bleed, die for the new Nicaragua—or for the old one?

How representative is Oscar Velasquez, a Managua welder, who says, "I'll do my part. If any gringo steps into my country with a gun, I'll shoot him if I can"?

Bismark Perez, a machine shop owner, says of the Sandinista government, "They want to strangle us." How far is he prepared to go to prevent what he perceives as his eventual ruination?

What of Modesta Martinez, of Ocotal, wrenchingly poor, illiterate, to whom the revolution has offered hope and dignity? She has leaped unquestioningly into "the process." "Last year I was the CDS leader in my barrio. Can you imagine *me,* with only one year of school, with such a responsibility?—I never thought I could kill another human being [but] I'm ready to kill to defend my country." How many Modestas are there among the "faceless" people of Nicaragua?

Yet there are those like the Casares fisherman who says clearly, candidly, "I don't understand anything about political things like the militia, the Sandinistas, that stuff. It doesn't interest me. It's not a part of my life."

How prevalent are the sentiments of Maria, a bitter young Miskito, who says, "You could say that the Sandinistas destroyed my family."?

Eusebio Picado, a Jinotega farmer, referring to the importance of his cooperative's new dairy herd, explains, "As a child I rarely saw milk—not me, not my father, not his father, going way back. For all of the *compañeros* here it was the same." How much is Picado prepared to sacrifice to keep his dairy herd?

Consider the confusion of Justos Smith, a Miskito forced by the tragedy of war and counterrevolution to evacuate his now-destroyed village on the Honduran border: "They tell me that the Miskito people have a good life in Honduras. But I know that Miskito people are returning from Honduras to Nicaragua. I don't know who to believe, what to believe."

Contrast Smith with Dania, a seventeen-year-old militia woman, veteran of seven years of clandestine and postrevolutionary struggle. "The militia, it gives meaning to my life. I'm in the struggle—I'm a part of history. That's the same as being immortal."

These are the people of Nicaragua. They are the subjects of this book, and they are the people who will determine their nation's future.

Although a small country, Nicaragua is by no means geographically or politically homogeneous. Consequently, this book has been organized into five distinct sections: Managua; The Countryside; Towns and Cities; The Atlantic Coast; and The War.

MANAGUA

Some 20 percent of Nicaragua's 3 million people live in Managua, the nation's capital. This city of 600,000 is the political, commercial, cultural center of the nation. Despite the devastation of the earthquake of 1972 (10,000 people killed, 600 blocks leveled), from which the city has never fully recovered, the population has doubled in twelve years. It is a metropolis without a *center,* largely lacking the charm and homogeneity of cities in other underdeveloped nations. Managua is *the* city, with strong foreign influences and a considerable professional and mercantile populace. It is the only Nicaraguan city that benefited from even a modicum of government interest during the corrupt forty-six-year Somoza dynasty. Managua is unique—it is a city-state within the nation. It is a metropolis apart, its people somewhat insulated from the war, the triumphs and failures, the struggles raging at this moment throughout the embattled land. It is in Managua that I found the softest support for "the process"—the greatest ambivalence among people of all classes.

THE COUNTRYSIDE

In the countryside the revolution has had its most dramatic and far-reaching influence. When, during the years of his tenure, Anastasio Somoza Garcia declared that where the people of Nicaragua were concerned, "I need oxen," it was the campesinos to whom he referred. Poverty, humiliation, illiteracy, disease, and degradation were the lot of the country people, who comprised more than half the population of Nicaragua. In the years following Somoza's defeat, the overwhelming, although limited, resources of the nation have been channeled to the countryside. It is here that the literacy, health, land distribution, and other programs have made their greatest impact. It was in the fields and the mountains that the long armed struggle was centered for most of the years of the insurrection. It is here that the greatest partisanship for "the process" exists.

CITIES AND TOWNS

In relation to Nicaragua's cities and towns, Managua is far and away *the* urban giant. The second city is Leon, with a distant 80,000 people. Granada, Masaya, Rivas, Esteli, Chinandega, Matagalpa—the half-dozen urban centers of city size—are considerably smaller. The remainder of the urban areas are, for the most part, peasant villages. Thus, while some 50 percent of the Nicaraguan people live in urban areas, the preponderance of them are country villages. Much of the population designated urban is actually rural, and attitudes and allegiances, particularly in the villages, are identical to those of their country cousins. Such industry as exists in underdeveloped Nicaragua is to be found, in large part, in these secondary cities.

THE ATLANTIC COAST

Zelaya, the vast department on the Atlantic coast, could almost be a nation in itself. Largely forested, Zelaya accounts for more than 50 percent of Nicaragua's land mass but only 8 percent of the population. The department of Zelaya is three times the size of El Salvador, with only one-thirtieth its population. Zelaya is *different*. Its people are predominantly Black, Creole, Indian. Its language is English; its religion, Protestant. Looking out toward the Atlantic, its culture is Carribean-influenced.

Traditionally, Zelaya and its people were considered a virtual Nicaraguan colony. Indeed, Somoza did not directly exploit Zelaya as he did every other area of Nicaragua. He was content, with some exceptions, to lease it to foreign interests. Its people and its timber, mineral, and fishing resources were largely exploited by foreigners—predominantly North Americans and British.

Zelaya's historical development and culture and attitudes are clearly different from those of the dominant Pacific coast Mestizos. The national integration of these independent peoples is a principal objective of the Sandinista government.

THE WAR

It is difficult to isolate the war from other aspects of Nicaragua. Indeed, the war and counterrevolution influence, to some extent, every person in the land. It is felt most directly in the border and rural areas of Nueva Segovia, Jinotega, Matagalpa, Chontales, and Zelaya. Here, there are frequent bloody raids by heavily armed, well-trained counterrevolutionaries. Most of the raids are incursions from Honduran and Costa Rican sanctuaries. Some emanate from hidden bases within Nicaragua, provisioned by air with U.S. direction and aid.

The counterrevolution is a war of destruction. Health facilities, sawmills, coffee groves and processing plants, food storage facilities are destroyed. Buses are attacked, isolated farmers murdered. Coffee and cotton harvesters are abducted, tortured, and killed. It is a conflict without boundaries or mercy. Its objective is to destroy the nation's meager infrastructure and to starve and terrorize its people into submission or dissatisfaction with their government.

The warfare is an integral part of the Nicaraguan story, shaping the thoughts and attitudes of the people. It is a story that must be told if one is to understand the people of contemporary Nicaragua. The soldiers and the men and women of Nicaragua's popular militia are Nicaraguan. They, too, have stories to tell. As the embattled nation's first line of defense, their convictions and motivations will considerably influence the immediate future of the nation.

The Nicaraguan revolution is under attack from many quarters. Partisans of the old status quo, both at home and abroad, are determined to reverse "the process" at any cost. Thousands of Nicaraguans, most often those to whom the past meant privilege, are at this moment engaged in bloody warfare. Other Nicaraguans, who for a variety of reasons will not countenance change, subtly and not so subtly lend their aid to the opposition.

No description of contemporary Nicaragua would be complete without mention of the role of the United States government. This nation is considered by the Sandinistas as the world's most aggressive and strongest imperial power. It rages at the very thought of social change. Arming, training, and directing the counterrevolutionaries; economic blockade; military provocations; threats—these are some of the means employed to bring down the fledgling "New Nicaragua." The U.S. government is despised by most in Nicaragua but hailed by some as a potential savior. At the same time, the United States is admired by most Nicaraguans for its wonderful technology and industrial development. Regardless of how one views the U.S., the "giant of the north" is never far from the thoughts of thinking Nicaraguans.

Regardless of what one thinks of Nicaragua and *Sandinismo,* it is undeniable that the Nicaraguan revolution is one of the great contemporary events of the Western Hemisphere. Indeed, the people of the poverty-stricken nations of all areas of the world are closely watching developments in Nicaragua. What happens in Nicaragua will considerably influence world history in the years to come. For that reason alone, the story of the people of Nicaragua has implications that go far beyond the borders of that small nation.

Unquestionably, my sympathies are not neutral. But in telling the story of the people of Nicaragua I have tried to be an honest reporter, interested in revealing the truth as I saw it.

NICARAGUA

The People Speak

PROLOGUE

War Comes to Ocotal

In the mountains of the north, in June, four A.M. is the blackest hour of the twenty-four. The first, the faintest light from the east is still one-half hour distant. At four A.M. in the clear air of Nueva Segovia the sky is a universe of stars.

It was almost one-half hour since the first rooster's scream had assaulted the still night air. Now he was joined by others, equally insistent. They demanded attention—harbingers of the day to come. The roosters were soon joined by the dogs. They bayed, they howled, they barked at the still brilliant moon, at shadows, at each other.

Yet, for the most part, Ocotal still slumbered on this Friday, the first morning of June. The country people of this border village clung to sleep.

In the rectory of Iglesia San Jose, the Catholic church, Joan Uhlen and Rachel Pinal, North American Maryknoll sisters, would sleep for another two hours before rising to begin their day's labor. Pastora, the lay Nicaraguan worker, was accustomed to the roosters and the dogs, as were the two nuns. They slumbered on. Mary Agnes Curran, a Franciscan nun just three days arrived in Nicaragua, was awakened by the predawn racket. She was excited at being in Nicaragua. She prayed that she would live up to her obligations; she feared for her ability to meet the needs of her ministry in the midst of war.

In barrrio[1] Sandino, Juana Maria Martinez, twenty-two-year-old mother of three, lay next to her husband, Raoul. Octavia, the nine-month-old, the youngest, whimpered, and Juana instantly awoke, rising on one elbow. Raoul was breathing steadily. The child became silent. The young mother immediately fell back into sleep.

---

[1] Neighborhood.

In the next house twenty-nine-year-old Maria Montalban was awake. She lay still, fearful of rousing the two older children by her side. Six-month-old Noel, she knew, would soon awake and demand the breast. Maria was thankful for the extra few minutes of rest. With Noel's first cry, she knew, her day's labor would begin, unbroken for seventeen hours.

Alberto Ruiz, too, was awakened by the roosters. The twenty-six-year-old turned and in the dim, moonlit room, smiled at his wife, Luisa, three months pregnant with her first. Her first, "a blessing," after four years.

But Ruiz, a laborer, could not dispel a nagging worry. Another mouth to feed. One more along with his mother and father and five younger brothers and sisters. As he did often lately, he shrugged off his doubts. "We'll manage," he told himself. "Everyone manages in the new Nicaragua. There's always a way." Unthinking, his hand went to Luisa's stomach. She awoke, smiling. Then they both lay back to await the dawn.

Armando Flores shivered in the chill night air. He offered a cigarette to his partner, Aurielo Chacon. They sat silently, smoking, on a pile of stacked timber. Aurielo glanced at the eastern sky. No sign of dawn. It would be an hour or more, he estimated, till the first men arrived at Maderero Yodeco, the sawmill. Then, their twelve-hour shift over, the watchmen could return to their homes—could sleep.

A pinpoint of light flickered in the ravine behind the cutting and conveyor shed. Flores nudged Chacon and pointed his rifle toward the light. The women of the Luis Alfonso Velasquez Cooperative were up, making tortillas probably, the surest sign that daylight would not be long in coming. Both men rose and continued on their rounds.

As always the day's work began too early to suit Marvin Lopez, the thirty-two-year-old director of the Ocotal IRENA, the Ministry of Natural Resources. He hurriedly kissed Elvira, his wife, and strode, preoccupied, through the door into the night.

A kaleidescope of thoughts troubled Lopez. The three women, the reforestation workers, were to meet him at the IRENA office. Would they be on time? Would the four others be waiting at Las Palmas? Had he remembered to fill the pick-up's gas tank? Had the seedlings been delivered yesterday as scheduled? What about the baby, Carlos' cough? Would Elvira remember to take him to the health center? Might Herolina or Cecilia catch the cough? Would they go to school today? Would Juan be waiting with the seedlings, the spades, the other tools?

Lopez turned the ignition key and the Datsun's engine responded immediately. He smiled. He frowned. Yesterday it seemed the front tire was soft. So many problems, he thought. So many responsibilities for a young man.

Nineteen-year old Juan Carlos Mendoza, his head cradled in his arms, lay dozing at the desk in the office of the Juventud Sandinista.[2] Julio Tercero smiled as he gently nudged the youth. Embarrassed, blinking, Juan Carlos apologized for having dozed off.

The two men shared *vigilancia*[3] at Radio Segovia. The building also served as offices for the Juventud and the CDS. Tercero, forty-two, was the CDS[4] director of Pueblo Nuevo, and he considered Juan Carlos as a son—another son, among so many.

Tercero was torn between waking the youth and allowing him to sleep. Juan Carlos was *special*—nineteen years old, soon to be married, a leader in the Juventud. A carpenter, but three nights a week a volunteer in *vigilancia*. He needs his sleep, Tercero speculated. But discipline—revolutionary discipline—was mandatory. He winked at Juan Carlos and forgivingly tousled his hair. Then he offered the youth an orange that he had been saving. Both smiled in understanding.

At four A.M. Eusebio Quadra shifted his rifle. The weapon was heavy, growing heavier every night, he reflected. Fifty-five years old, the father of eight and another on the way, Quadra, as he was wont to do these days, thought back upon his life. The years as a farm laborer. Now a security guard at Beneficisco De Cafe Pedro Altimarando—the coffee-drying and processing plant. This is better, he thought, especially for a man my age. At my age one can no longer labor in the fields. He longed for his lost boyhood; but . . . he enjoyed this work. Coffee, production, he told himself. Nicaragua's life.

Across the road Quadra made out the dimmest outline of INE, the electric company office. Beyond the office building the ridge the forest, the mountains, Honduras.

Quadra heard the sound of an auto engine. He rose quickly and removed the rifle from his back. Then he saw the IRENA pickup truck. That would be Marvin Lopez. Good. The day wasn't far off.

---

[2] Young Sandinistas; Nicaragua's principal youth organization.

[3] Neighborhood block watch. Residents organize to patrol or to watch for "antisocial" behavior. The *vigilancia* is credited with dramatically reducing street crime that had been so prevalent in the past.

[4] Sandinista Defense Committee—the principal mass organization in Nicaragua, with branches in neighborhoods and workplaces.

Quadra waved as the truck drew abreast. But Lopez, preoccupied, apparently didn't see him. The three women sitting in the back, in the truck bed, did, and they waved. Quadra returned to his thoughts and his work.

Two kilometers beyond the coffee-processing plant was the sawmill entrance. Lopez drove by the gate, and in two minutes was in the countryside. He drove quickly on the Carretera Ocotal–San Fernando.

So far-so good. He sighed. Apparently he had been unnecessarily concerned about the tire, and the fuel gauge registered almost full. This will be a successful day. The three women had been on time. They had been waiting for him. All is well.

That was Lopez's last thought, marking the end of his existence on this earth. A single bullet from an M-16 crashed through the windshield and into Marvin Lopez's forehead. He never heard the sound, nor did he feel the pain. He died instantly.

The truck continued for seventy yards along the gravel road and at the first curve crashed heavily into a slight brushy incline. It fell to its side, the wheels turning madly. The women were thrown to the ground. They had heard the shot. They saw the dark forms—the contras—by the roadside, and they ran, terror-stricken, into the forest.

A quarter hour later, at 4:30, Aurielo Chacon stopped for a moment at the sawmill gate. A few minutes earlier he had passed Armando, the latter walking slowly toward the machine shop. Both had nodded and passed, wordless. The shift was drawing to a close. Once again, thank God, it had been an uneventful evening.

And then the explosion. The world of Aurielo Chacon burst into fire and flame. As Aurielo turned toward the saw and conveyor shed 200 yards to the east, he felt the earth beneath him tremble. Grenades, mortars, automatic rifle fire blasted the summer night. The sky turned red.

Unthinking, he ran toward the chaos. Then, in silhouette, he saw them. Flitting shadow forms. Were they twenty, forty, a hundred men? He paused and Flores was by his side.

Now, from their left, a roar in the auto-truck repair area and then a burst of flame. At the same instant the administration building exploded and collapsed.

What to do? Where to go? Aurielo Chacon dropped to one knee and started firing wildly in the direction of the machine shop. Flores saw the running, fleeting forms of men near the administration building, and he, too, blasted at the shadows. Surrounded on three sides by flame, mortar fire, grenades, both men fired frantically at the running men.

Flores emptied his clip and jammed in a replacement. Chacon did the same, and then he shouted, "It's a storm, a nightmare!" Now the entire sawmill was ablaze. From every quarter came the thunder of mortars and bombs.

Flores rose and gripped Chacon's shoulder. "There's nothing more we can do here. Nothing." The two men rose, walked, and then ran through the gate toward the road.

The town of Ocotal awoke to the sound of carnage at the sawmill. During the following moments it was gripped by panic, rage, anger, fear. They were under attack. By whom? How many? Where? No one knew. But each reacted in his own way.

Alberto Ruiz threw himself from his bed and grabbed the trousers lying on the stool alongside. Luisa, three months pregnant, took his arm. He shook her off and now, wearing only his trousers, rushed to the rifle standing against the corner wall. He threw the sack of ammunition clips across his shoulder.

"Your shoes!" Luisa called.

"I'll be back," he shouted.

As he ran through the door, Alberto heard his wife's plea: "Alberto, be careful!"

Ruiz was in the militia, and 100 yards from the house was the *granero,* six grain storage silos, Ocotal's food supply for the coming months. A prime target, he knew, for destruction. He ran cursing toward the silos. He knew the others would also rally to defend the granary.

Ruiz breathed a sigh of relief at the sight of men advancing on the silos. "That's revolutionary vigilance," he half-muttered proudly. "The *compáneros* are here—even before me."

Then, stunned, he realized that these running figures were not *compañeros.* These armed men were *them.* He raised his rifle and fired wildly toward the contras. Then a dozen automatic rifles were turned on Alberto Ruiz. In an instant he fell, torn and twitching, to the ground.

With the sound of the first explosion Raoul and Juana Martinez sprang from their bed. They had often discussed the fact that Radio Segovia, in the adjoining building, could be a target for a contra attack. The two swept up their still sleeping children. They laid them on the floor, alongside the bed.

The children cried in terror, and Juana Maria whispered comforting words as Raoul threw his body over them.

A moment later an explosion rocked their flimsy, wooden house. Shrapnel ripped through the thin wall, and a ragged piece of steel tore into Juana's back. She screamed and then lost consciousness. The babies howled. Raoul took Juana Maria into his arms. He rocked her, beseeching God to spare the lives of his wife, his children.

In the adjoining house Maria Montalban, too, awoke with the sound of the first explosion. She reached over to touch seven-month old Noel. The older children screamed. As Maria started to rise from her bed a bullet pierced the wall of the house. It shattered her right ankle, tore through the length of her leg, and exited at her hip. As she passed out, the last sound Maria Montalban heard was that of her screaming children.

Next door a force of forty men attacked Radio Segovia. The heavy wooden door was easily breached by two grenades, and a half dozen more were thrown through the windows and into the entryway. The building was overrun by a horde of screaming contras. In a moment they overwhelmed the stunned, bleeding Julio Tercero and the boy, Juan Carlos Mendoza. Both were badly wounded, their bodies pierced by grenade splinters. They lay motionless, groaning, on the stone floor.

One of the invaders grabbed the older man's collar, raised his head, and put a bullet into his temple. A second rushed in with a gallon can of gasoline found in an adjoining room. He emptied its contents over both men and set them ablaze. The youth screamed in agony for more than a minute. Then he was still.

Eusebio Quadra, at the coffee processing plant, sprang to his feet as he heard the explosions. At the same time, across the road, he spied a body of men rushing down the hillside toward the electric company office.

Quadra stood motionless for a moment and, then, as the figures grew distinct, fired at them. The return fire was withering but, miraculously, Quadra was untouched. He turned and ran to the administration building to make a stand against the forty or fifty men he estimated to be in the raiding party. Quadra covered the thirty yards in seconds and threw open the door to the darkened building. As he did so, a bullet severed his spine. He fell dead in the doorway. Five minutes later Quadra and the coffee-processing complex were in flames.

The nuns and Pastora, the Nicaraguan lay worker, were awakened by the first dull explosion at the sawmill two miles distant. Minutes later, the granary, barely one-half mile from Iglesia San Jose, erupted. Plaster dust filtered through the air as the women gathered in the hallway of their house.

Was this the long-expected invasion? A contra raid? An air raid? The questions were unending. They had no answers. They prayed. Sister Joan noted with satisfaction that the new one, Mary Agnes, was cool, calm. She will be fine, the more experienced nun thought to herself.

Now the explosions came from every section of Ocotal. Automatic gunfire and bombs thundered through the night.

Joan had been through similar situations during the insurrection of 1979. But she often said, as one doesn't get accustomed to the imminence of death. The electricity was out. So, too, they soon learned, was Radio Segovia. The telephone, though, was still working. Rachel made a phone call to the Maryknoll mission in Leon. Hers was perhaps the first message to the world that Ocotal was under attack. Amidst the warfare raging beyond the door, the sisters gathered drinking water, bits of food and clothing. Then, like the people of Ocotal, they prayed and they waited.

It was still dark, still night, in Ocotal.

At 4:30 A.M. the first feeble cast of daylight insinuated itself over the embattled town.

Five minutes later there began the first feeble, fragmented defense of the town of 21,000. Local militia men and women, armed night-watch people, sought and found one another. In groups of three, five, fifteen, they sought out the invaders. The small unit of regular Sandinista military—perhaps forty in all—assembled.

But the contras—and their firepower—were overwhelming. It was later established that more than 500, divided into six commands, had invaded Ocotal. During the night past they had walked in over the mountain, from Honduras, eight hours distant. With surgical precision they had destroyed their objectives, and now they dominated the streets of Ocotal. Every scattered, tentative challenge to their power was quickly, mercilessly overwhelmed. The people of Ocotal cowered behind closed doors, awaiting the storm's end.

At 6:15 a bright new day had begun. But the stench and smoke of battle hung over the bleeding city. The first cautious Red Cross medics had ventured out to collect the casualties. Here, the broken body of a twenty-four-year-old mother of two lay face down on the pavement before her house. There, a seventy-two-year-old grandfather, shot through the throat as he sat on a rocker with a child on his lap. There, a seven-year-old girl and her younger brother, now mute, deafened by a mortar explosion.

The first of the wounded were carried across shoulders, in autos, in jerry-built stretchers, in handcarts to the hospital.

Raoul Martinez rigged a stretcher from a bedsheet and two spade handles. Then he ran into the street and flagged down a fourteen-year-old militiaman. Together they carried the unconscious Juana Maria to the hospital. The two older children, carrying their nine-month-old sister, followed behind.

Maria Montalban, her leg shattered, lay in her blood-soaked bed. From time to time she awoke to the sound of her children's screaming. And then, perhaps mercifully, she lapsed into unconsciousness.

Luisa Ruiz, expressionless, sat on the ground alongside the body of her dead Alberto. Two hours earlier he had been warm, vital. Now he was a still, cold corpse. Dry-eyed, muttering to herself, Luisa, unknowing, numbed, patted his blood-matted hair. Her hands and her night dress were soaked with her husband's blood.

The nuns of Iglesia San Jose ventured out into the street. They visited a neighbor, a large panic-stricken family, and offered what they could—comfort. Scattered gunfire still wracked the streets. Pastora, hugging the walls of buildings, walked to the Centro Desarrollo Infantil, her place of employment. "Maybe I'll be needed there," she insisted.

Amidst the gunfire a young girl, perhaps fifteen, walked through the streets, a bullhorn to her mouth. She called for blood donors to report to the hospital.

Elvira Lopez, spurred by a dread premonition, ran through the nearly deserted streets, begging passers-by for information of her husband. Five miles away, on the Careterra San Fernando, Marvin Lopez lay lifeless in the cab of the IRENA Datsun.

A helicopter roared overhead, and once again the town was convulsed by fear. Honduran? Yankee? It was Nicaraguan, come to survey the attack. Twenty minutes later the first of a convoy of the Sandinista military sped into town from the south. The battle shifted.

The invaders regrouped and retreated to the mountains, to the sanctuary of Honduras.

Now, as the Nicaraguan military pursued the enemy through the forests, the gunfire, the explosions, came from the north. The cleanup, the catharsis began. The injuries would be patched, the bleeding staunched. The grief-stricken would be comforted and the dead buried. On this day the war on Ocotal would find temporary surcease. The wounds would be a long time healing.

1
MANAGUA

The Sandinista Capital—Nerve Center of "The Process"

> These times are different. The present time is
> not like those in which Sandino and his
> beautiful guerrillas battled alone against the
> Yankee Empire.
>
> —Carlos Fonseca

Saida Rugama is thirty-nine. She is a secondary school teacher. Rugama is handsome, tall for a Nicaraguan woman. She is precise in her choice of words, articulate, and forceful.

In our barrio, Bello Horizonte, we have three CDS organizations. On our street we have Bello Horizonte Number One. Others are Number Two and Number Three. We've been looking for a good name for our committee—the name of a martyr of the revolution. For five years we've been considering different names. I don't think that we'll ever choose one. We're always so busy with other things.

Our barrio is a working-class neighborhood—you might call it middle-class. We have twenty-two houses on our street. That's 110 people, including children. Many of our neighbors work for private institutions. Others, for the government. We have teachers, social workers, office workers, an agronomist, some small shopkeepers. My husband works for UNAG, the organization of farmers and ranchers. We have four children. In our CDS I'm the secretary of organization.

Our organization was established before the Triumph,[1] during the insurrection. Then, it was called the CDC—the Civil Defense Committee. We worked to defend the people against the Somoza dictatorship.

[1] July 19, 1979—the date of the Sandinista victory over Somoza, also referred to as the Triumph of the Revolution.

The CDC was clandestine. It was dangerous to oppose Somoza. At that time we had maybe eight members on our street. There were other people who were very good, very sympathetic. But we only admitted the most committed, the most trustworthy.

We did what we could to protect, to strengthen, to unify the people. We did what we could to resist Somoza, to prepare the people to bring down the dictatorship.

For instance, we collected medicine and foodstuffs for the fighters and for our future needs. We oriented the community about how to protect themselves against attacks by Somoza soldiers and airplanes. We constantly talked to our neighbors to raise their political consciousness.

We had "safe houses" to shelter our *compañeros*.[2] During those days many were hurt or sick. Others were hiding from the Guardia.[3] We sheltered them, we nursed them, we did what we could.

Sometimes there were city-wide demonstrations against the dictatorship. Then we banged on pots. We made noise to demonstrate our solidarity.

Sometimes the Guardia announced that they were going to make a sweep of the neighorhood to clear it of "Communists." They ordered us to vacate the neighborhood so that they could search every house, every street. We urged our neighbors to remain. Some did; others were frightened and they left.

After the Triumph we continued our work. But now we became the Sandinista Defense Committees. Now, of the twenty-two families on our street, nineteen have one or more members in the CDS. Of course, some are more active than others. It depends upon their level of political understanding, their commitment to the process, and, of course, to personal considerations. Some people have two jobs or they attend school at night. So they don't have the time.

For instance, we have all been active in the health campaign and in the *vigilancia*. In the old days, if a person's house was broken into, that was *his* problem. No one cared. Now, if such a thing should happen, the entire neighborhood would be involved. It's the same thing with an illness or a death in the family.

In our neighborhood, during the rainy season we have a problem with floods. So the CDS makes sure that sewer drains are kept clean

---

[2] Comrades. *Compañero* is also used to denote a person with whom one lives.

[3] The national guard; Somoza's military force.

of debris. Together we paint the curbstones, we prune the trees—things like that.

Of course, as I said, some members don't want to or can't participate too much. But we keep them informed anyway. Our job is to keep the people informed. If they don't participate, okay, maybe next time. No hard feelings. We didn't win our revolution with hard feelings among the people.

Our CDS sponsors many neighborhood fiestas. For instance, the Day of Happiness. That's on July 17, the day Anastasio Somoza left Nicaragua. It's a national holiday. We make a piñata for the children. We distribute candy. They play games. Everyone has a good time.

On Mother's Day we made a big cake. We had a party for all of the mothers on our street. We had it right on the street.

Then our CDS celebrated Purisima. That's a national holiday commemorating the conception of Jesus. It's an eight-day holiday, and it ends on December eighth. On Purisima we built an altar for the Virgin Mary. We had fruits and candy for the children. There were games and entertainment. It was very, very successful.

This is the sort of thing our CDS does. We keep very active. Our organization meets about once a month—sometimes more, sometimes less. It depends upon the needs of the time. About twenty or thirty people attend—which is considered to be good attendance. We hold our meetings in the street. Everyone brings a chair and we meet outdoors—it's cooler outside. That's the way things are done in Nicaragua. Of course, sometimes it rains. Then we all go to someone's house.

Our CDS is growing, growing, growing. The political consciousness of we Nicaraguans is growing, growing, growing. The process—I'm convinced that it's irreversible. Our CDS—it's a school. It teaches us to leave our social sicknesses behind.

———— ♦ ————

In the poor Managua barrio of Maria Auxiliadora is the Escuela Maria Auxiliadora. A crude wooden home has been converted to a sewing school, primarily for neighborhood women. This is a project of the trade union CUS.[4] In the large room are six or eight crude tables used to lay out and cut patterns. There are perhaps fifteen sewing

———

[4] Confederation for Trade Union Unification. This trade union, affiliated with the Social Democratic Party, is in opposition to the Sandinista government.

machines, donated by the Canadian government. There are no charges here save for materials used by the students, twenty of whom are hunched over their machines, cutting patterns, chatting with each other and with their teacher. One of the students is Ligia Garcia, a stocky, dark, animated woman of forty:

I'm a Managua person. I was born here. I raised my family here. But no more. Now we live in Tipitapa. That's about twenty-four kilometers[5] east of Managua. I come to the school three-four days a week, and believe me, the bus, the materials, they cost me a fortune. But maybe it'll pay off. I hope so.

We lived in Managua until the earthquake, until 1972. When the earthquake hit, the whole house fell down. The roof, it fell right on my bed. If my husband and I had been in bed then, we'd be dead today. Every day I give thanks that none of my children—I have eight— were killed in their beds.

After the earthquake my husband borrowed a truck. We piled everything we had left on that truck. We put the kids on top of our sticks of furniture and left Managua. We went to Tipitapa, to my husband's family.

I said, "Never again. I'll never again live in Managua." To this day I get nervous when I'm in Managua. You have to live through an earthquake to know what I mean.

Life for us is hard. It's no paradise. For me it's very hard. My husband drives a truck for Perfecta, for the milk company. But now half of the trucks aren't working. They're broken. They say they can't get the parts to fix the trucks, and so the trucks sit on the lot, broken.

So half the trucks aren't working, and neither are the drivers. My husband, Arturo, works only half the time, like the trucks. You can't live like that. I can't go to the market and say, "Let me have the rice for half price because my husband only works half the time and only earns half pay." They'd laugh at me.

Arturo earns now about 3,000 cordobas[6] a month. And it costs me 150 cordobas a day to feed my family. You figure it out. Impossible.

That's why I come to this school—to earn some money. I used to buy scrap cloth, odd bits and pieces. I used to make little short pants for children. A friend of mine would sell them for me in the Mercado

---

[5] About fifteen miles. A kilometer is six-tenths of a mile.

[6] At the official rate of exchange—about 3.9 cents per cordoba—this is roughly $117.

Oriental. They paid me 12 cordobas for each pair of pants, so I was able to make a little something for my family. Now I can't get the scrap cloth, so I'm out of business.

I'm learning to make dresses, skirts, blouses. I'm learning to embroider. When I get good enough I'll make women's clothing to sell. It'll be a help to us. That's the way you have to live today in Nicaragua.

Life for me is hard. Harder, I think sometimes, than in the earthquake. At least then no one bothered you. I have a son. He's seventeen years old, and he's gone. That's right. He's gone. He ran away to Costa Rica. He doesn't want to be in the army. So every couple of days, two or three times a week, *they* come to my house to look for him.

I say, "Come in. Look. Look. Look under the bed. Look behind the oven. Maybe he's hiding there." They look and then they go away. And then they come back again. It's hard for me. Hard, hard.

I have another boy, fourteen years old. Now I'm worried that they'll try to take him. I don't know what I'll do.

To feed a family today in Nicaragua, to protect your sons, it's very hard indeed. For poor people life is very difficult. It always has been. It always will be.

———— ◆ ————

Francisco Ramon Chavarria, twenty-seven, is an electrical engineer. Chavarria is a slender, intense young man. As he talks he drums the table with his fingers.

I was born in Jinotega. My father was at the university. He was a professor of biology. My mother was illiterate, a campesina.[7] They were never married, but they had four children together, me and my three sisters.

He never did anything for my mother or for us. When my mother was pregnant with my youngest sister, he married another woman.

I'm not bitter toward my father. He was what he was. He was from another class, another time. If I passed him on the street, I wouldn't look at him. But then, neither would I strike him. I feel nothing for him. Not hate, not love—nothing. After the Triumph of the Revolution he went to the United States. That's good. That's where he belongs. I believe he's working in a university there.

———

[7] Country woman.

When I was growing up we were very poor. My mother supported us by washing clothes for other people. She worked by the day in the fields. She worked hard. Work was all that she knew—work and her children and her church.

I always worked. When I was nine years old I sold newspapers on the street. My father's father had a big farm in Jinotega. Sometimes I worked for him. During the harvest seasons we all—my mother, my sisters, and I—we all worked for him.

When I was older, maybe fourteen, fifteen, I worked in a coffee processing plant. I paid for my school with the money I earned there.

After the Triumph of the Revolution I moved to Managua. I attended the Nicaraguan Technical Institute—ITECNIC. I was trained as an electrical engineer. After graduation I got a job, a good job. Now I work for the government. I'm responsible for the delivery of electricity to a sizeable portion of Managua.

Why did I choose this field? Because, frankly, I wanted to do something useful for myself and for my country. I served Nicaragua during the revolution, and I'm serving Nicaragua today. Electricity is important. It's the foundation of a technological society, right?

I work for the city of Managua, and I belong to a union, the National Union of State Employees. It's affiliated with the CST.[8] But I must admit that I'm not active in the union. Why? Because there aren't enough hours in the day. Let me tell you how I spend my time. First of all, I work six days a week. Then, I'm a musician. I play percussion in a band. I'm a militant in the Juventud Sandinista. I'm in the militia. And I'm active in the base committee of the church in my barrio, Le Reinga.

Chavarria frowns at a question regarding a possible contradiction between his role as a Young Sandinista and as a church activist.

Our band plays at church functions and at Juventud Sandinista affairs as well. There is no contradiction. So-called "contradiction" is a lie that is spread by people who refuse to see the reality of Nicaragua. I mean Monsignor Obando[9] in the first place.

Obando is screaming to the Pope to get the priests out of the government. Why? Because when we have D'Escoto as foreign minister and Cardenal, as minister of culture, both of them priests, and all

---

[8] Sandinista Workers Confederation; Nicaragua's major trade union.
[9] Archbishop Miguel Obando Bravo, bishop of Managua.

of the other priests in the government, it is a message to the world that we are not anti-Catholic, only anti-capitalist.

Why does Obando hate the Sandinistas so much? Because he's lost his privileges. Now he has to pay taxes like everybody else. His rich patrons—they've lost their privileges. They say that we Sandinistas don't respect religion. That's the grandfather of lies.

Our people are Catholics—strong Catholics. But we don't believe in a church that doesn't believe in justice. We don't believe in a church that willingly allows itself to be used by foreigners, by the Yankees, to destroy our nation.

Look at it this way. The hierarchy—Obando Bravo—has enough power to stop the intervention. But how does he use his power? He wants us to engage in dialogue with the counterrevolutionaries. He wants us to sit down and talk calmly with our murderers—those who destroy our food, our schools, our churches.

I ask you, Who are the true Christians? Obando Brando and the hierarchy or we Sandinistas, who are trying to build a new society, a just society?

Look, I get excited about this question. Let me tell you something good. My old mother—now she lives here in Managua with one of my sisters and her family. My mother is busy enjoying her nine grand-children. And you know, they are all very Catholic and all support the revolution. So you see, there is no contradiction.

———— ◆ ————

Brief discourses by two Managua cab drivers:

We Nicaraguans have short memories. We forget too soon what it was like before, especially for the kids. Sometimes a boy or a girl was against Somoza. Then, in the night there would be a knock at the door. The Guardias would take the kid. The next time you saw him was in the morgue. That was for the lucky parents. Others they never saw again. I know. I had a daughter. She was sixteen years old . . .

They're crazy, the government. What will we get from Russia? What has Russia got? Nothing. Now, the United States—it has everything. Rich, powerful. The United States has always taken good care of Nicaragua, right?

———— ◆ ————

Edgar Antonio Santana, thirty-eight. Santana is slightly-built, unshaven. There is a bitter edge to his tone, and he is eager to talk with a foreign writer. Santana is a mechanic-machinist.

I've been working in auto repair shops and machine shops in Managua since I was sixteen years old. That's twenty-two years. I started at the bottom, as an apprentice. The first place I worked, where I learned the trade, was a shop called Silva-Re. A very good place. They're still in business.

I'm very experienced, very skilled. I know machines and engines inside-out. I have a certificate from a company in the United States, Federal Mogul, attesting to my mechanical skill.

My wife and I have six children—three boys, three girls. My oldest daughter, Flora Dalia, is a secretary in the Ministry of the Junta. My fifteen-year-old son, Luis Alberto, is in Cuba. He got a scholarship to finish secondary school there. When Luis returns to Nicaragua I think that he'll be prepared to make a good living.

That's important, because at this moment things are worse here than at the time of the earthquake. We have trouble getting everything, even the necessities. You can't get milk, meat, cooking oil, medicine. And when you get it, the price is crazy. A pen, a little pen, it costs 80 cordobas. A pen used to cost 6 cordobas.

I think that the reason the prices are so high is because the shopkeepers hold back. Look, they have three cans of oil. They'll sell two and hold one because they don't know what will happen tomorrow. They're speculating. They're hoping to get higher prices. They want to make big money.

Also, the government spends too much on the military. That raises prices. You see, the military gets priority for milk, rice, meat—everything. That causes shortages, and that causes the price of everything to go up.

Things are disgusting—worse than the earthquake. I'm not crazy for the Sandinistas. I'm not one of those people who say they're crazy for the FSLN[10] just because they're the boss now. But I don't know any party that's any better. It's the same monkey, but with a different tail.

———— ♦ ————

[10] The Frente Sandinista—the National Liberation Sandinista Front.

Opinions on a variety of subjects by two Managua attorneys. Attorney A is fifty-three years old. He is dark, squat, volatile. Attorney A's specialty is criminal law. Attorney B has just turned seventy. He is of medium height, slender, fair. He wears horn-rimmed glasses and tends to be somewhat reflective. He is in commercial law.

On the Sandinista government

A: This is not a free country. I dare not give you my name because I could go to jail for ten years, for twenty years. We live under Communism. Totally. Fidel Castro owns Nicaragua.

B: Nicaragua is not Communist. Not yet. We still have some private business here. But we're too close to Cuba, to Russia. Soon we'll have Communism.

On Somoza

A: I prefer Somoza one hundred times to this Communist government. Except at the end. Somoza was pushed too hard. He had to push back.

B: I must agree that I had more freedom under Somoza. Except at the end. He wanted to be a king. He wanted to pass the power on to his son. That wasn't right.

On freedom of the press

A: We have no free press. Definitely not. Oh yes, we have *La Prensa*. But if they say something the government doesn't like, they shut it down. The press was much freer under Somoza.

B: I listen to the Voice of America. The Germans, the Dutch, the BBC also have good Spanish-language programs. So I know what's going on. But I don't think the press was freer under Somoza. It was bad then. It is bad now.

On counterrevolutionary activity

A: They wish to bring down this Communist government. I say good luck to them. The sooner, the better.

B: I'm not in favor of the contras. They're attempting to destroy the economy, and that's bad.

On literacy, health, and other Sandinista social programs
A: I don't believe it. I don't believe anything they tell us.

B: [A negative wave of his hand indicated that B didn't wish to comment.]

On the economy
A: No matter how much money you have, you can't buy anything. There is nothing here. Before, there wasn't a thing you couldn't buy in Managua if you had the money. *[He pulls out a roll of bills.]* This is worthless.

B: Take toilet paper. At the government stores the price of a roll of toilet paper is 8 cordobas—if they have it. So you go to the free stores, and three rolls of toilet paper costs 100 cordobas. That's a lot of money.

On the United States
A: A wonderful country. We always had good relations with the United States, and I'm sure that they want to, still. But the Sandinistas are Communists. What did we ever get from Russia or Cuba? I lived in San Francisco for seven years. I'd go back in a minute.

B: It's true that the United States has always helped us, and wants to, still. The Russians and Cubans have nothing. I studied law in Switzerland and France and then at New York University, in New York City. That was right near Washington Square Park. That's a beautiful park. New York is a beautiful city. I think it's the capital of the world.

On the Nicaraguan elections
A: How can we have free elections? We live under Communism.

B: I'm not so sure. But they give the vote to sixteen-year-olds. People that age don't have enough experience to vote properly. And they allow soldiers to vote—soldiers in the barracks. Do they allow soldiers to vote in the United States?

On the future, assuming that the war ends and the economy improves
A: I still want to leave.

B: I don't know. It's pretty hard to live in a strange country. If our economy improves . . . Well, we'll see.

———————— ♦ ————————

Tobie's Ferreteria is a Managua landmark. One of the city's largest hardware stores, it is perhaps the best-stocked and most successful. The proprieter, Rollin B. Tobie, is a Black man. He is forty-six years old, erudite, worldly, soft-spoken. Tobie is widely known as a civic leader, successful businessman, and as a social and political critic and activist.

Do I believe that I have a future in Nicaragua? Look, a myth has been spread that we Coast people are lazy, without ambition, don't care to work, and so on. So, to prove a point and, incidentally, because it's a good investment, I decided to go into the cattle business. I established a ranch, a big place near Bluefields. It was virgin land, and I started from the very beginning. In 1981 I bought the land, I had it cleared, and so on. I bought some stock. Now it is starting to produce. Someday it will be very successful. It was a sizeable investment, but it will pay off. Do I have confidence in my future in Nicaragua? What do you think?

This government has made tremendous efforts, particularly in the areas of health and education. But in matters of the cultural needs of the people of the Atlantic coast, of the traditions and history of our people, it has failed. I know. I speak as a Black man. I was born in Zelaya, in the town of Bonanza, in 1938. My father was a miner.

From the beginning the Sandinistas have mistrusted us. We are Black and Indian. We have a different history, culture, religion. We even speak English, a language foreign to the people of the Pacific coast.

And the interesting thing is that we are all victims and inheritors of imperialist traditions. Here on the Pacific coast they have an inheritance of Spanish imperialism. We on the Atlantic side had British imperialism. Yet we are all Nicaraguans.

Perhaps if we had shared the revolutionary experience, things would be different. Perhaps if we had lived under the same oppression as the *Spanish* . . . But you see, under Somoza there was a laissez-faire attitude in the Atlantic zone. Certainly we were exploited—our gold, our timber stolen from us. But politically, culturally, Somoza ignored us.

**CDS meeting at the
Roberto Huembes
Market, Managua**

There was a major war here on the Pacific side. Tens of thousands
gave their lives in the struggle against Somoza. On the Atlantic
coast, very little.

Then came the Triumph—and the Sandinistas. They didn't know
us. They didn't understand us. They didn't want to know us. To them
we were foreign—Indians, Creoles, Blacks. We were, in their eyes,
enemies or potential enemies. They feared us as potential counterrevolutionaries. It wasn't so much a matter of racism. Racism as it exists
in the United States has never been a problem in Nicaragua. Certainly, there have always been differences based upon class and
wealth. But otherwise, we Nicaraguans tend to live and let live.

The attacks from Honduras certainly made the problem worse. But
the Sandinistas made no secret of their contempt for us. They bullied
us, they jailed us. Specific cases? Here's one, not earth-shaking, but
typical: Some Miskito mothers visited their sons who had been
imprisoned on various charges. The Sandinista guards insisted that
Spanish be spoken. The poor women couldn't speak Spanish, only

Miskito. So they had to return, many miles and days of travel along the river and through the bush without having talked to their sons. Another case: Many Spanish-speaking people in the Bluefields area are now wearing T-shirts embossed with the slogan "Atlantic Coast Culture is Imperialist Culture"—in English! What in insult!

I've heard of other, far worse, examples. But these simple practices demonstrate their insensitivity to us—their contempt.

So now we Nicaraguans, all of us, are paying for this. There is considerable counterrevolutionary activity on the Coast, particularly among the Miskitos. Before the Triumph we had few doctors, engineers, teachers, or other professionals. Now we have less. Most of them are in exile—in Miami, New York, Costa Rica. It's not that they are counterrevolutionary. It's simply that they've suffered ill will and chose to leave Nicaragua.

The rest of the Coast people, most of them, don't participate in anything. They have an "I don't care" attitude. They simply sit and watch events. Certainly they make no contribution to the defense or growth of Nicaragua.

I personally have always believed in investing, and I've never been able to simply sit and watch events. I told you of my ranch in Bluefields. Well, I also have a farm here near Managua. We grow corn, pepper, fruit. And I have a stable, too. I bought some Peruvian horses. Beautiful animals. I'm going to breed them.

I don't believe in simply accumulating money. It should be invested. It should be made to work. I believe that when I make these investments, I show confidence in the future of my country.

It has been proven that bureaucrats make bad administrators. They tend to look at politics rather than at profit and loss. The social aspects of the process are fine, but at the same time you cannot be losing money forever. These people aren't fools. They know this. They want Nicaragua to prosper, and to do so, those who wish to work must be allowed to do so. Those who wish to invest in our nation must be permitted to do so, and to profit by it.

As a businessman, I think that I've been investing both for myself and my country. Look, during the war and immediately after the Triumph, many people in my business, the hardware business, got frightened. They got nervous. They didn't know how the future would treat them. So they decided to dispose of their businesses and leave Nicaragua. All right. I decided to remain. So I bought a lot of merchandise at very good prices. As a result, I have a very large stock. Who benefited? I benefited. Nicaragua benefited.

Everything that happens in Nicaragua today is colored by the war. Everything must be viewed within that context. Look, our problems here, especially on the Coast, are intensified by the war, by fear. Other, *new*, problems are coming into being because of the war. With the war's end, things will settle down. We'll have a chance to breathe.

The United States must leave us alone. I don't think that the United States' talk of "democracy" and "liberty" has much credence in Nicaragua. Traditionally, the United States has supported regimes in Latin America that snuff out democracy and liberty. They don't have good credentials.

Negotiations with the counterrevolutionaries? Perhaps that would be possible if the counterrevolutionaries weren't led by Somocistas. But, negotiations with the Somocistas? Never.

I was here during the war. I saw the boys and girls running up and down the streets with guns. I saw what the Somoza people did to innocent people—the torture, the murder. I don't think it is realistic to expect Nicaraguans to sit down and negotiate with these people. The people won't have anything to do with Somoza's henchmen.

I'm optimistic, though. I believe that in the end justice will triumph. We will have peace and freedom in Nicaragua—far better than before. But first, I'm afraid, there will be much more suffering.

One week after this interview, the counterrevolutionary radio, broadcasting from Honduras, announced that Rollin Tobie, "traitor," was slated for "execution."

———— ◆ ————

Visiting the office of the stridently anti-Sandinista newspaper, La Prensa, *I struck up a conversation with a woman who was typing in the outer office. She appeared to be in her early forties. She was very fashionably groomed and dressed.*

I work here at the *La Prensa* office two or three afternoons each week. My husband is an attorney and he's very busy. I like to keep busy, and so I work here. I don't work for the money. Money's not worth anything in Managua today. You can't buy anything.

You say that money's not worth anything now. Tell me, how has your life changed since the Triumph?

Don't ask. You know, we used to have a marvelous orchestra in Managua—the Managua Symphony Orchestra. Now its gone.

Campesino near Somoto, Madriz

Where did it go?

Who knows? They couldn't pay the musicians, so they left Nicaragua. There's no money for good music today. Today everything is *folklorico.*[11]

What do you think of the literacy campaign?

It's good that they're teaching those people to read and write. I have no social life.

[11] Folk music.

No social life?

No social life—nothing. My friends—they're all gone. They're in Miami, Costa Rica. I have no one, nothing left in Managua.

Do you plan to remain in Nicaragua—to build a life for yourself and your family?

Who knows? Sometimes I feel like a stranger in my own country. It would be impossible for you, a stranger, to understand.

———— ♦ ————

The Mercado Oriental is Managua's principal market. It is the city's oldest and largest. The Oriental is similar to markets throughout Latin America and elsewhere in the world. It is vast, with acres of stalls, booths, stands. Many are in one large building. Others are outdoors under the relentless tropical sun or rain. These are often protected from the weather by jerry-built awnings, umbrellas, and scraps and bits of canvas.

Everything needed to sustain life can be bought at the market: chickens, rabbits, ducks—live or dressed; hardware and electrical equipment—new or used; clothing; food of every sort; charcoal; toys; stationers supplies; furniture; hammocks; pharmaceuticals; haircuts. The vendors tend to be tough and aggressive. They often articulate the thoughts and hopes of their countrymen.

Maria Carmen, thirty, rents a small stall in the market. She sells women's clothes. Her entire stock—perhaps twenty dresses, skirts, blouses—is on display, hanging from the booth's ceiling and walls.

I've been working in the market for seventeen years. I have no husband, no *compañero*, so I provide for my mother and myself. I had only four years of school, and I worked to help my family since I was a child.

Before the Triumph it was the same. I worked hard then. Long hours. I still have long hours and I still work hard.

But I'll tell you something. In the old days, the police, they wouldn't let me live. They ate my flesh. It was always pay, pay, pay. Then, too, I was a young girl. They took my money—and they wanted a bonus. It was very hard for me. Very hard for all of us in the market. Especially the women. Especially the girls.

Now it's different. It's more fair. Look, I'm not a political person. But I think that this government wants to do the right things. In things like the police and the schools and the health campaigns you can see the difference.

There are many things that we can't get now, that we used to be able to get. So sometimes it is difficult. But maybe it will be better when the war is over.

At least now the police leave me alone. To me, that's the most important thing.

———————— ♦ ————————

Brief conversations with three young women, classmates, all studying to become primary school teachers:

Lesbia Patricia Chacon is sixteen years old. She proudly presents her card: Carnet de Militante 003995, 21 de Septiembre, Juventud Sandinista.

I'm a Sandinista, and both my brothers are, too. So are my mother and my father. He's an artist. You could say that we're a Sandinista family.

We're all in the militia, too. We train together. We're in the same unit. It's nice when the whole family is together like this. We're all of us together, training, preparing for whatever happens.

Look, I like the North American culture. I like the music, the movies, the television, the clothes. I like the North American people. You're a North American and you're all right. But I'm a Nicaraguan and I'll fight for my country. I really hope that we don't have to fight the North Americans.

Lesbia's friend Eva is eighteen.

Politics? I don't know. You see, there are ten brothers and sisters in my family. And my father, he's very strict. I don't know how he feels. We don't talk about these things in my house.

Me? I'm young. I like to sing. I like to dance. I'm studying to become a teacher. I want to live. That's all I know.

Her friend Betty, eighteen, is a Salvadoran and pregnant.

My mother and my father are school teachers. Three years ago, in El Salvador, we got word that my mother was being *watched*. The next day she packed our bags and—we four children, two boys and two girls—she took us out of the country. My father stayed behind in El Salvador.

My husband is Salvadoran, too. He and my mother work here in Managua, in the El Salvador solidarity movement. I, myself, I'm waiting for my baby to come, and I'm studying to become a school teacher.

My older sister is in Costa Rica with her husband and baby. I have a brother in Mexico. Our little family is in four countries, and my baby will be born in a foreign land. We need to be together. We need to go home to El Salvador. Someday we will.

———— ♦ ————

Mario Lopez Diaz is twenty-three years old. Tall and broad for a Nicaraguan, he has curly black hair and an engaging smile. Lopez has been teaching himself English, and he is pleased to practice with a North American. We met in the Mercado Roberto Huembes.

My mother owns this business. She makes *nacatamale* [yucca, rice, bits of beef, tomatoes, served on a broad banana leaf]. She's not rich, not poor. She earns enough to keep the house. This young woman, helping, is my girl friend. My sister-in-law, she helps out sometimes, too. It's a living.

I work in the meat section. I'm a butcher's helper. I don't mind working in the market, but really, I'm a boxer, a fighter [he displays his knuckles, swollen and discolored]. I'm very good. Very strong. Very fast. The problem is, you can't make a living as a fighter in Nicaragua. I want to go to Mexico or Costa Rica.

Would you like to go to the United States?
Certainly.

Guatemala?
If I could make a living as a fighter there.

Honduras?
Same thing. If I could make a living there.

El Salvador?
Yes [pause]. Maybe it's too dangerous in El Salvador. Maybe Mexico or Costa Rica would be best. I'm a good fighter. I could be a champion.

———— ♦ ————

Angela DeValdivia, thirty-nine, is a housewife. She is carefully groomed, very attractive. She is soft-spoken and seems somewhat preoccupied—fragile even.

My husband, Jaime, is very enthusiastic for the process. But I, myself, I don't know.

Jaime is an economist. He works at the bank. When he talks to me, when he explains, then I believe that we needed the changes. But at other times, I'm not so sure. You see, I'm not a political person.

I was born in Matagalpa. We had a large family—twelve brothers and sisters. My father was in business, and we were very comfortable. There were many, many poor people, and life was very unfair to them. They needed the revolution, but we—me—no. Now we have the war and that is horrible. All of these young men are being killed—horrible!

I sent my twenty-two-year-old son out of the country. He's in Costa Rica, at the university. He's studying to become an engineer. It would be impossible for Adolfo to study in Nicaragua. All of the excitement, all of the turmoil. A student needs peace, tranquility. I insisted that he go, that he get a good education to prepare himself for a career. After all, he has his whole life ahead of him—isn't that so?

Then, of course, I worry that if he stayed in Nicaragua, the military might take him. So you see, a mother has much to worry about.

We in Nicaragua should be permitted to solve our own problems, and this aggression must be stopped. Of this I'm certain. But at the same time, I must admit that sometimes I'm frightened by the revolutionary process. All of these poor people—ignorant, uneducated—they're being stirred up. The parades, the speeches, the meetings, the demonstrations. I don't know what will come of it all.

———— ♦ ————

In Managua's Oriental Market I stopped for a soft drink and a bit of shade from the bone-shriveling heat. Two young men, a driver and his helper, sitting in the cab of their truck, eyed me, exchanged a few words, and then approached.

Are you an American? Do you own a car? What kind?
I'm an American, and I own a Japanese car.

What kind of Japanese?
A Toyota.

That's a good car, right? How much does it cost? In dollars.
It's a nice car. It costs about $9,000.

Do you own a motorcycle? How much does that cost?
A new motorcycle costs about $2,000 or $3,000, I think. I don't know much about motorcycles. I never owned one. [I decided that it was my turn to ask some questions.]
Are you a Sandinista?
The banter over, the young man regarded me solemnly.

No. I'm not a militant. But I'm *not against* the Sandinistas. I'm *for* "the process," the government.
Why?

Why? Because now I'm a man. Before, we were nothing. There are some walking the streets today who would like to go back to the old days. They *say* they're against Communism, that they're for democracy. But, no. They want working people on their knees again, at the bottom. They think we're stupid. But we're not stupid. We're smarter than *they* are.

———— ♦ ————

Marina Isabel Mena de Cano is forty-one years old. She is attractive and meticulous in her dress and her grooming. She tends to be nervous, animated.

Marina Isabel Mena de Cano

I was married at seventeen, here in Managua. At twenty-six I was a widow with two little children. My husband was an accountant, a good man, ten years older than me. But nine years after our marriage he got cancer, and he soon died. When my husband died, my life changed very much.

I was born in Juigalpa, in the department of Chontales. When I was little we moved to Managua—my father, my mother, my two sisters, and I.

We lived on a farm in Chontales. We had cows, chickens, horses. It was a very nice life as I remember it. My mother was a schoolteacher. She taught primary school in Juigalpa. Later she did the same here in Managua.

My father died soon after we came to Managua. But our lives didn't change. We seemed to have enough money, enough of everything. My sisters and I went to school, we helped our mother in the house, and then I got married.

Soon after my husband died I bought this house. We had some money saved, and with insurance and other benefits I invested in this house—a place to keep my family together. For me, though, everything changed. Life became very difficult for me.

This house was a good investment. It provides a part of my income. I rent rooms. I have private little apartments around the garden. It's really quite nice, pretty, isn't it?

I rent mostly to foreigners. Last month I had an artisan, an Italian who taught in a school in Granada. After him, a Guatemalan. Once I had an Arab—a Libyan. He was a good cook. He made delicious Arab food. But mostly I have students, sometimes journalists from the United States, Germany, England. Most stay for two weeks or a month. But they must pay in dollars. Cordobas, they're worthless.

I have a profession, too. I design clothes—skirts, dresses, blouses—anything for women. I have a seamstress who comes three days a week, and she makes clothes from my designs. I sell to neighbors, friends, friends of friends—like that. My clothes are expensive. But today, everything is expensive—if you can get it.

Take meat. You can't get meat. The butcher store opens at nine o'clock. At four-thirty, five o'clock in the morning people start to line up in the street to get meat. Lorena, who works for me—or sometimes I myself—stands in the line when it is still dark.

Milk. Before you could get all of the milk you wanted. Now try and get it. What are they selling? Powdered milk. It's terrible. I go to a farm three mornings every week to buy real milk. You have to be there at four-thirty in the morning when they milk the cows. It's expensive, but at least it's milk.

I know a farmer who has many chickens. Sometimes I buy eggs from him. I sell them to my neighbors. In that way I make a few cordobas. That's the way life is today. I'm always planning. I'm buying, I'm selling, I'm waiting in line. I'm going here, going there. Anything to get what we need; anything to earn a few cordobas. It's very difficult. I hate this life.

Everything costs. People don't realize. I have light and water bills, taxes. I have to give something to Lorena. The gardener comes every two weeks. He must be paid. I have problems with the plumbing, the electricity. Tomorrow an electrician is coming to fix some lamps and repair the wiring. God knows what he will charge. My car is six years old, and it needs repairs, parts, tires. It's impossible.

And food. I have a big household. I have my mother—she's eighty years old—my daughter, Liseth, and Lorena. My nephew Armando lives with me. Armando is a student. He lives in Granada, but he goes to school in Managua. Liseth and Armando work, too, and they help out a little. But food, impossible.

Liseth is studying psychology, and she wants to go on—to continue her schooling in Mexico. But for that you need dollars. Who has dollars?

Me? I have no recreation, no social life. The only enjoyment I have is four or five mornings a week I go to my exercise class, and I jog, too. That's my recreation. You have to keep fit, right?

I have worries, many worries. My son, Paulo, he's twenty-two, and he was married last year. He works in a bank—he's a lovely boy. Now I'm afraid that they're going to take him into the army. If they try to take him, I don't know what I'll do.

I don't vote. Not me. To hell with them. None of them are any good.

———— ♦ ————

Liseth Mena is Marina's daughter. Liseth is twenty-three years old, a student. An attractive brunette, she is vivacious, candid. Her blue jeans, tennis shoes, T-shirt are in sharp contrast to her mother's formal dress.

My life is full. I'm always busy, always in motion. I attend the university full-time and I work full-time. Don't ask me when I sleep.

I go to La UCA—the University of Central America. I think it's a good school. My major is psychology, and I'm in the fourth year of a five year program. One more year to go. I like clinical psychology, but

Liseth and Paulo Mena

I still don't know whether I'll specialize in children or adults. I'm interested in both. We'll see.

After I graduate from UCA I'd like to continue my studies. I hope to go to either the University of Mexico or to East Germany. I think I'd prefer to study in Germany. I hear that they're doing very interesting things in clinical psychology.

Of course, money is a consideration. It's possible that I can get a scholarship to study in East Germany. I'm trying. I'm working very hard to get a scholarship.

My job—it's wonderful. I work at the Reeducation Center Campesinas del Cua, right here in Managua. We have about thirty patients, all girls between twelve and fifteen years old. They had all been prostitutes, thieves, things like that. I work four nights a week, from seven in the evening to six in the morning.

The name of the center, Campesinas del Cua, is symbolic. Cua is the name of a Nicaraguan village. In this village, in Cua, all of the women had been violated by the Somocista Guardias. There had been a garrison in that town, and all of the women had been raped, many times.

Like the women of Cua, our patients, too, have been violated. They've been violated by a legacy of injustice, of exploitation.

We stress that at the center we do not *rehabilitate*. We hope to *reeducate*. Rehabilitation? For what? In Nicaragua there is no longer any institutional injustice, exploitation, repression. We aim to *reeducate*. We want to open their minds to the opportunity for the rich, productive life that is now possible in our country.

First, we have formal education. Everyone must master the basic skills: reading, writing, arithmetic. Then, we teach work skills. Some of our patients learn sewing. Some, those who are so inclined, we send to commercial and trade schools in Managua. Some have even been sent for advanced training to Cuba and other socialist countries.

My work—I'm called an *educadora*. I do group dynamics. I supervise games. I lead group discussions about their personal lives, about the news of the day, about national problems—anything, everything. The main thing is to help them to think about things beyond their previous limited experiences. Also, we must help them to learn to express themselves. I observe them—even while they sleep. That's when I get *my* sleep—sometimes three or four hours.

I love my work. It fills me with happiness to know that I'm doing something important, something for society. I feel that I'm building for myself, for my people, for the revolution. I feel myself growing, learning all the time. That's a good feeling.

In Nicaragua the future is beautiful, especially for the poor people, especially for the children. We're getting opportunities that we never had before.

My mother—she's a good person and we respect each other's views. She's a good woman, and she has many problems, financial and otherwise. But she comes from a different time. She is a strong individualist. She sees everything from a very personal point of view. She has not yet developed a collective outlook. So it is very difficult for her. Maybe she'll change. For her happiness, I hope so.

———— ◆ ————

Julio Cesar Garcia, twenty-one, is a machinist. He is a bright, articulate young man. Rather small in stature, he seems older than his years.

I'm a machinist here at the El Progresso Machine Shop. My ambition is to someday be a very good machinist—to own a place like this.

I started working here six years ago when I was fifteen. I began as an apprentice and I've been working my way up. I'm learning the

UNAG office, Masaya

business. I want to become an expert in every aspect of machine-shop work.

As I said, my ambition is to own a machine shop, but that's very difficult. These machines are very expensive. I'm trying to save money, but you know how things are. It's difficult, very expensive in Nicaragua. It's almost impossible to save money.

But I'm trying. I wouldn't be satisfied to be a foreman or a manager in a big machine shop. That's the same as being a worker. I don't want to be an ordinary worker. I want to be the boss. One thing I learned. You've got to look out for yourself, right?

In the meantime I don't mind working here. I make a living—more or less. I make 8,500 cordobas a month. But the money doesn't go far. There are four brothers and sisters in my house, plus my mother and father. That costs me something. Also, I have two kids by a woman, and I have to help support them.

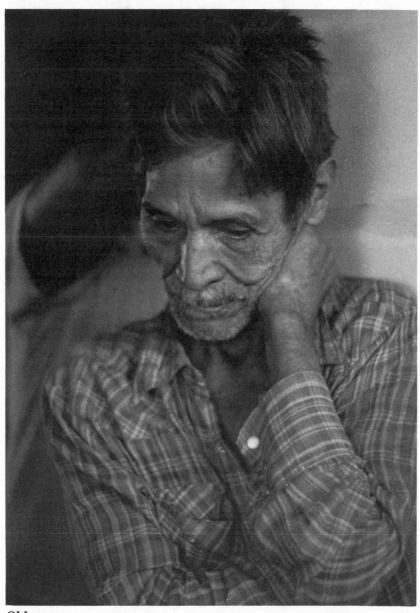

Old man

One of my brothers works here. He's a foreman. My other brother is an auto mechanic. He works for the Ministry of Health.

I must admit that things are better in the shop since the Triumph. For instance, we have a lot of heat and smoke. It used to be miserable. See that ventilator? We have four of them. We got the first one right after the Triumph. They help. It makes the place less hot and smoky.

Also, we get more money now, more bonuses and better benefits—things like that. We here are all in Simaresa, the machinists' union. We're affiliated with CUS. I'm active in the union. I'm the secretary of finance. We have twenty-five members in the shop.

But the most important thing to me is me, myself. I want to get ahead. I don't want to be a simple worker all of my life. I want to get ahead, to be a better man.

Will I realize my ambition? Who knows? Life is very insecure for me in Nicaragua. This climate of war makes me very uneasy.

First, we need peace. Then we need other countries to help us. Every country—not only from one side. You see, Nicaragua is a small country, a poor country. Without help we cannot survive.

Everything is so insecure, so up in the air. That makes me very insecure about my life, my plans. Getting married now or really saving money for my own shop is out of the question.

I don't get involved with things that don't affect me personally. I wouldn't go into the militia, for instance. I don't like the military—it's just not for me. Then there's the draft. If they called me, I don't know what I'd do. How can anyone know until it happens to him?

I worry about the war, about the invasion. I think that we have to have negotiations—with everyone, even with the contras. After all, they're Nicaraguans, too. If Nicaragua was invaded by the contras, I would be neutral. If we were invaded by Honduras or by the United States, I would fight—I think.

After all, you have to do what you yourself believe in. You have to look out for yourself, right?

———————— ♦ ————————

Bismark Perez Cabezas, thirty-four, is Julio Cesar Garcia's employer. He is a partner and the manager at El Progresso Machine Shop. Perez is an intense young man, preoccupied and wary of a foreign stranger.

We do reconstruction work here. On engines. Seventy percent of my business is the reconstruction of engines for trucks, autos, trailers, motorcycles.

The work we do is very important to the nation's economy. Especially now, in Nicaragua's present situation. You see, Nicaragua doesn't have the dollars to buy new, so must repair and rebuild what we have. Most of the engines that we work on used to be scrapped, thrown out. But now we fix those engines. We keep them working.

In Managua today you could count the shops like this on the fingers of your hands. There is a terrible shortage of machine shops. We ourselves, we could double or triple our volume of business overnight. The business is there. In our situation private industry has the will and the ability to expand. That's on the *one* hand.

On the *other* hand, the government doesn't *want* us to expand. You see, we need more machinery, and today all commercial relations are on the basis of the dollar. We go to the government office and they're very negative. They say that Nicaragua doesn't have the dollars to buy the parts and new machinery abroad. Is there such a shortage of dollars? I don't know. I do know that dollars are squandered on things that are not so necessary to our economy. Guns, for instance. Also on other things that don't provide any return.

I started this business eleven years ago. I'm in partnership with my brother. Today we have thirty-one employees, including administrative people. Look around you. See the machinery? Since the Triumph we haven't bought one piece of machinery. Nothing. Some of our machines are from the United States, some were made in Spain. Most is from Denmark. I think that the Danish make the best. But never mind. I would take machinery from any nation in the world to expand—to meet our potential in the market.

Another way the government is hurting us is with the war. Help is a problem. We can't get workers. We used to start our people as apprentices of fourteen, fifteen years. They started sweeping the floor, cleaning the machinery, helping the machinists, doing simple jobs. In three, four, five years they became skilled machinists.

Now you can't get young people. Half of them are in the military. The other half are hiding. They stay home, they won't come out of their houses, they won't take a job. I don't know. Now, even if by some miracle we got the machines, maybe we wouldn't have the manpower to operate them.

We have problems that are unbelievable. See these saw blades? Small parts like this, we have to go to Costa Rica and smuggle them in.

I'm not a political person, but really, I'm not in sympathy with this government. Of course, they've probably done some good things. They talk a lot about the social programs, but really, that's just public relations for the world to see.

The root problem is that the government simply doesn't want private business such as mine to grow. They want to strangle us.

I'm a businessman and I don't like politics. I admit that I don't know much about politics, nor do I want to. But sometimes life's experiences force you to think about these things. The war, for instance. No one wants war—it brings no benefits. So we have to end this war at any cost. We have to bring about an understanding among all Nicaraguans. That means sitting down and talking with the so-called counterrevolutionaries.

The Sandinistas say that without the United States aggression there would be no war. But I don't think so. Even without the United States, the fighting would continue.

In Nicaragua today we have no freedom of religion, of expression. We need pluralism. We need to become the real democracy that our fathers told us about.

I'm not a political person, but I honestly believe that these are the problems we face. The first thing this government should do is start negotiations for peace with all of the parties. Then it should demonstrate its respect for pluralism. It should help private enterprise to grow instead of placing obstacles in our path.

———— ♦ ————

Gilma Yadira Tinoco, thirty-one, is vice-dean of the Humanities Department of La UCA, the University of Central America. As we talked in her small office, there were constant interruptions—students and professors dropping in with questions and comments. The phone rang frequently, exciting bedlam.

I was a student here at the University of Central America during the last years of Somoza. Later, at the time of the Triumph, I was on the faculty. I also did graduate work in the United States, at the University of Washington. So you see, I know this place well. And I'm fascinated by the changes.

UCA is a Jesuit institution. Traditionally, it had been a college for the rich, the children of the very wealthy. The National University, also in Managua, was considered to be a school for the middle class. For the children of the workers, farmers, the poor, there was no higher education in Somoza's Nicaragua. Now, of course, that's all changed.

In Somoza's Nicaragua I was a part of the privileged class. My father was an attorney—a founder of the Social Christian Party. He's retired now, inactive, but he still likes a good fight. There are fourteen in my family, and we cover the political spectrum. When we are together, we fight plenty. But we have respect for each other. That was one thing my father taught us—respect for each other's opinions.

There are 10,000 students at UCA—4,000 in the Humanities Department. That's about the same enrollment as before.

This is still considered a somewhat elite school, but now we get more students from the middle class and the working class. The National University is broader. It has special programs for workers, campesinos.

Tuition is not a problem here or anywhere in Nicaragua. The cost is nominal—about 138 cordobas—at every university in the country. Of course, it's all subsidized by the government.

Before the Triumph we had a unique situation at UCA. Many of the professors were sympathetic to the struggle. Many of the students were Somocistas. So the professors had to be careful. To develop a reputation as an "anti" could mean discharge or even imprisonment.

There was always a small cell of the Frente at the university. But they were limited because the repression was so strong. So the level of political thought here was low. The students, for the most part, avoided any political expression or activity. Their level of political understanding was very low. They were, in large part, politically, socially, asleep.

Now, of course, that has all changed. Our students *live* politics. Talk, talk, talk. They breathe politics. Forty or fifty percent are in the Juventud Sandinista. Some of our students are apolitical. Some are against the process. But at least these things are discussed—they can be argued about. It is wide open. This is now an exciting place to be.

Students here used to be interested only in their own personal careers, nothing else. That still exists—it would be a lie to say that everything has changed. But now there is a great deal of interest in the nation's needs as well. Students still come to get a degree, to get a profession, to make money. Personal interest still exists, but at the same time there is an ever greater involvement with the social needs of the nation.

You see, there is a tremendous shortage of university-trained people in Nicaragua, so there are many opportunities. Many of our people, by the time they are senior students, are working in their chosen professions—and at the same time attending classes.

Many of our students are in the militia—they are called up from the classroom and go off to the frontier for three, four, or six months. When they return we make special provisions for them. These students receive special tutoring, and they are permitted to take their examinations as though they had been here the entire time. These students are more mature, more resourceful. They add a new, good dimension to the student body.

This is a wonderful—and a terrible—time for young people. Some of our students don't return from the frontier. Many have died in defense of the country.

Since the Triumph of the Revolution the University has had many problems. Some of them are really exciting problems. For example, our entire curriculum has been adapted to the new Nicaraguan reality. Before, much of our thought was copied from other countries, especially the United States. Now we emphasize our own history and culture.

This has meant the need for new textbooks, teaching materials. There had always been a serious shortage of teaching materials in Nicaragua. Now the shortage is even greater.

After the Triumph much of the faculty went to work in the various government ministries. Other specialties went to work in industry, in the reconstruction. There had always been a shortage of teachers. Now it was even worse. So we've come to depend more and more upon graduate students to teach undergraduates.

Also, teachers' wages were too low, so we lost many, many good people. It took two years to accomplish, but finally university professors got a 50 percent increase in salaries. Primary and secondary schoolteachers' salaries were increased 100 percent. The base pay at the university is now 10,000 cordobas a month. That's not a great deal of money, but it's an improvement.

This is a good place to study, to work. It's exciting, stimulating. I come home at the end of the day to my husband—he works at the Ministry of Transportation—and to my two-year-old twins, and I'm exhausted and excited. It's a good feeling—like you're really alive.

———— ◆ ————

A brief conversation with a slight, handsome twenty-six-year-old student:

Although my father was Guatemalan, I consider myself Nicaraguan. I was born here in Managua, and my mother was Nicaraguan. So that makes me Nicaraguan, right?

I attend the Institute, and I study agriculture. But I'll never work in that field. I'm going to Canada [From his wallet he withdraws a frayed business card: "The Good Earth Natural Food Store" in Vancouver.]

I have a friend who is going to get me a good job in Canada, helping to build houses. It's true, isn't it? Canada's a big, rich country like the United States, right?

───────── ◆ ─────────

Oscar Velasquez, thirty-one, is a welder. He works in the huge lot of the Ministry of Construction. Scattered about the lot are scores of trucks, tractors, bulldozers, awaiting repair. Velasquez proudly conducts me about the lot, point out newly repaired, freshly painted machines on which he has worked. He is a bright, articulate, enthusiastic young man. He is of medium height, husky, with a broad, open face.

Oscar Velasquez

We had fourteen children in my family—fourteen who survived. My mother, I know, had more. I'm not sure how many died. My father was a campesino. He worked around El Crucero—that's about twenty-four kilometers south of Managua, on the road to Carazo.

I had six years of primary school. But then my father abandoned our family. I was the oldest, and I left school to help my mother in her work. She sold *chicha* [a corn beverage] in the Mercado Oriental. She still sells *chicha*. But now she's in the new market, the Roberto Huembes.

I got my first real job in a small shop as an apprentice welder. We made iron gates, window frames, doors—all ironwork for homes, commercial buildings, factories. This job paid only 2 cordobas an hour. But it was a help to my family. And of course, I learned my trade there. I worked in that shop for three years.

Next, I worked at Metassa Iron Works. That was a big place. It was owned by a partnership of the Somoza family and some North Americans. We made materials for construction—beams, trusses. We even built small bridges. There, too, the pay was horrible. I started at 2½ cordobas an hour, and at the end of three years I was earning a "big" 4 cordobas. We worked from six in the morning to seven at night, six days a week. That was seventy-eight hours a week.

One thing at Metassa was very good. We had the best equipment, good tools. That makes a job much easier, pleasureable. But the long hours and the low pay were horrible.

One time a couple of guys tried to establish a union at Metassa. That was forbidden in those days. Those guys were fired. Maybe they were arrested. I don't know. I never saw them again.

After the Triumph of the Revolution I got a job at Albert Elia. That place was owned by Italians and North Americans. Here the pay was much better. We got 10 cordobas an hour—20 cordobas for overtime. At Albert Elia the work was much the same as here. We did repair and maintenance on heavy machinery—bulldozers, tractors, trucks, buses. The problem at Albert Elia was that it wasn't steady. When there was no work they laid us off. One time when I was laid off I came here, to the Ministry of Construction.

Working here at the Ministry of Construction is okay. It has its good points and its bad points. The pay here is good. I work on production and I earn 3,000 cordobas a week. That's good money. Also, it's secure. There are no layoffs. We have a good health-care program, and at our cafeteria we get a good meal for 6 cordobas. The same meal in a restaurant would cost me 60 cordobas.

We work nine and a half hours a day, five days a week. We have a good union—the German Pomares Ordones. It's affiliated with the CST. They try. They do the best they can.

What I don't like about the job is the *tortugismo*. I'll explain: You know how slow a *tortuga* [turtle] is? Do you get it?

We have a shortage of everything—oxygen, acetylene, grinding stones. I know about the economic blockade. I know all about that, but there's more to it.

I'll give an example: We need grinding stones. So *they* go out and buy stones—*polishing* stones. Now, I know that there are grinding stones in the market. But *they* buy *polishing* stones. So we use the polishing stones for grinding. And in fifteen minutes, a half hour, they're ruined. So the job is held up while *they* go out and buy more polishing stones. It's not as though they don't know the difference. These guys have been here twenty, twenty-five years.

So we have meetings and everybody talks about it. And nothing happens, nothing changes.

I'm not accusing anyone of sabotage. That's a strong word. But some of the old-timers, some of the foremen, they're not exactly in love with our revolutionary process.

I'll give you another example: A boss here got drunk and he smashed up a new eight-cylinder pickup truck. That's a half million cordobas. So what happened? Nothing. They cover up for each other, see?

I think it's not going to change. They're not going to fire these guys, because they know the work. They know the shop, the process.

Maybe Mother Nature is going to rescue us. They won't live forever. They're going to retire someday. But in the meantime? I't's a worry. Some of the younger guys, we talk about it. We worry.

For me personally, for my family, things are much better. But I worry about the process, about the country.

Two years ago the government gave me a piece of land, a building lot in Barrio Nueva Libia. It was free. The land cost me nothing. I built a house for my family. I have three children and my wife is expecting another any day. The house isn't too good yet, but I'm working on it. It's getting better all the time.

I attend school at night. I'm in my fifth year of secondary—the last year. I started going to school soon after the Triumph. You see, I used to be a drinker, a heavy drinker. But then things changed here. I saw real possibilities for a future for myself. I stopped drinking and I started to go to school to better myself. Now I'm thinking, "Hey, some day I can be the boss here." Then when we need *grinding* stones, we'll get *grinding* stones.

I used to be the CDS coordinator in my barrio, but I had to give it up. My work, my school—it was too much. I didn't have the time. My wife started to take over as coordinator, but when she got pregnant she didn't feel too good. I think that after the baby comes she'll start again. Meanwhile we both still do *vigilancia,* though.

Last year was hard for us. I'm in the militia, and I was mobilized for six months. So it was financially hard for us. I continued to get my base pay but no production pay. You don't get production pay when you're not actually working on production.

One thing I notice lately—all the foreigners in Managua. That's good. Maybe when they see what we're trying to do they'll go home and stop the aggression.

That's what we need—solidarity. We need worldwide solidarity to stop imperialism. I know I'll do my part. Any gringo steps into my country with a gun, I'll shoot him if I can.

Jose Maria Garcia Castro is a student. The twenty-year-old youth seems to be bursting with energy, enthusiasm. He is anxious to talk of himself and his country.

It's impossible for me to say how and when I get involved with the political movement. When I was fourteen I became active in the Christian community. So the base of my engagement is from a Christian point of view. I think I became a Christian first. Then I became a revolutionary.

My three older brothers were active in the revolution—in the Frente. One of them killed in the insurrection. His name was Juvencio Amed. Juvencio was nineteen years old, and he had been fighting for three and a half years.

My parents, of course, suffered great pain from his death. We all suffered when Juvencio was killed. But I think my parents—all of us—were prepared for this tragedy.

Harvesting coffee. Las Manos, near the Honduran border

At first my parents were nonpolitical. They were frightened by the danger to their sons. But they grew. They became very strong. My brothers were always talking politics. And in my home, during the insurrection, we were in constant contact with guns and bombs. I think that this helped prepare my parents for what happened to Juvencio.

Now I think that we Nicaraguans are a new people. For the first time the Nicaraguan people are making their own history. Our parents and our grandparents and those that came before them, they didn't make their history. Others, the rich and powerful, made our history. Foreigners, Yankees, made Nicaraguan history. Our people were just instruments. We were used.

So you see, these are my thoughts. To me they are political and they are religious. To me they are the same thing. I'm very active in both, and it's hard for me to separate my religion for my politics.

Take my job: I have a part-time job while I attend school. I work as the distribution manager of *El Tayacan*. That's a weekly newspaper with a Christian point of view. It's sold throughout Nicaragua, even in the schools. *El Tayacan* supports the process, but it's privately owned. It's not published by the government.

My main work, though, is my school, my education. I attend the Industrial Technical Institute. I hope to become a mechanical engineer. My wife, Sandra, she's studying agricultural administration. It seems like the entire country's going to school, right?

We're all so busy. I'm so busy. That's why I'm not as active in the political movement as I'd like to be. Even so, Sandra and I are both in the Juventud Sandinista, and I'm in a militia unit. Sandra is in the health brigade in our barrio, San Luis. We're both preparing for the United States invasion. I'm ready to fight for my country. I'm at peace with myself and with God.

All of my family are Christian except one brother. He doesn't believe in God. That's no problem. Not for me, anyway. He has the right to believe or not to believe, according to his conscience.

I'm not a Marxist. Not because I disagree with it but because I don't know enough about Marxism. We Nicaraguans should take the best pieces of Marxism and use it to build a just society. Nicaraguans should learn from all revolutionaries. We should take what's good and leave the rest behind.

For instance, take Allende. We learned from his mistakes. Allende left his military intact, and see what they did to Chile. We learned a lesson from that. We destroyed Somoza's National Guard.

We've had much help from Russia. And the Cubans have been very helpful, too. The Russians and the Cubans—we've learned from their successes and their failures. Nothing is perfect, right? The important thing is that we must go forward.

———— ♦ ————

2
THE COUNTRYSIDE

Rushing Into the 20th Century

Peasant learn to read
Peasant learn to study
Peasant if you read and study
The ground you cultivate will be yours
—Jorge Issac Carballo

SEBACO, MATAGALPA

Our auto proceeded slowly down the rutted, hard-packed dirt road. The small mud, stucco and planked houses on both sides were rough, unfinished-looking. They seemed fitter, though, than many we've seen in this poor countryside. Many had new zinc roofs, and the bits of wooden trim—doors and window frames—had been recently painted.

Naked toddlers hovered close to their mothers as the latter stared at us, expressionless, from open doorways. The ever-present mongrels of all sizes wandered aimlessly along the dusty road of this hamlet. Pigs and chickens rooted, foraged, and pecked in the thin grass alongside the road.

There was a flimsy wooden bridge at the road's end, and we drove cautiously over it. Along the roadside just beyond the bridge was a large circular sandbag fortress. Four armed men lounged casually against it. One, an AK-47 pointed vaguely in our direction, detached himself from the others and signaled us to stop. He approached the auto. The guard was middle-aged. He wore the rough clothes of a campesino. Hatless, unshaven, his eyes narrowed as he peered into our auto and asked our business.

Twenty pairs of eyes were fixed on our auto as we talked. Wordlessly, he motioned us to proceed.

The administration building of the Leonel Valdivia Cooperative is identical to the houses we had just passed. Perhaps it's a bit larger. Three curious children followed us inside.

The floor—hard-packed dirt—was swept clean. At the far end were two desks. Two dozen crude chairs and benches lined the walls. On those rough walls were neatly posted clippings from Barricada *and* Nuevo Diario. *On the walls, too, were large Frente banners, posters pictures of Sandino, Fonseca, and other revolutionary heroes.*

As we entered, three men were seated by one of the desks, talking. One of them, the oldest, approached us. He is Inginio Palacio Alaniz, the education director of the Leonel Valdivia Cooperative. Palacio is a tall man, forty-eight years old, with a shock of reddish brown hair. He greeted us with a tentative smile. Then he introduced the others—the director of finance and the director of operations. Both appeared to be in their twenties. We mentioned the tension in the village and Palacio responded apologetically.

We had a little trouble, and our people are cautious. Eight days ago *they* threw two grenades at the building. They destroyed a truck out front. We can only thank God no one was hurt. There are always people around. The children are in and out of this building like their homes.

I'll be happy to talk to you, to answer your questions. Maybe you'll learn something about Nicaraguan cooperatives. But there are many far more advanced than ours. Others, they're not so far along. All of us, we're learning. We learn something new every day.

How old is the Leonel Valdivia Cooperative?
On the fourteenth of July we celebrated our fifth anniversary. That makes us five days older than the nation.

How is that possible?
This section of Matagalpa, the area around Sebaco, was liberated five days before Managua was. As the Guardias were beaten, as they threw down their arms, the people came and took this land. They established the cooperative.

How many people established the cooperative? Were you among them?
One hundred and twenty people from this area liberated this land and established the cooperative. I was not among them. At the time I was with our military forces. Many of our present members didn't take part in the liberation of this land. They were occupied elsewhere in Nicaragua.

Banana plantation worker, Chinandega

Has the membership been consistent?

Now we have only forty-eight members. You see, many of the original members weren't campesinos. They were mechanics, drivers, carpenters, people of many different occupations. Most of the campesinos remained—others joined later. Now we have forty-eight members—forty men, eight women.

Only eight women?

Until last year we didn't admit women to membership. You see, this work is very hard here. It's all hand work—stooping, kneeling. We thought it was too hard for women. But we saw that women were working very well on other farms in the area. Some of our members wanted to include women, and so we voted on it. The majority was for women membership.

Who owned this land before?

Before the Triumph it was owned by several people. The largest parcel was owned by a Somocista named Farjar Zamora. The church owned a small parcel.

You just took the land?

Why not? The Somocistas ran to Honduras, Miami, Costa Rica. So the land was just here. All it needed was someone to work it—that was us. The land that belonged to the Church—it was donated to us. The rest . . . [he shrugs].

Can anyone become a member of the cooperative?

Yes, if they've had experience on the land or if they're willing to work, to learn. But we've found that some of the others, those who weren't campesinos before, have other ideas. Some of them want to become businessmen. We're careful. Our members must have a cooperative attitude. They must have a socialist spirit. We're not entrepreneurs. We're campesinos, militants, building a new nation based upon justice.

How do you decide who can belong?

All potential members are auditioned by our membership. Everyone who wishes to join must study our regulations. He must understand them. He must agree to them. Then he has a two-month period to make certain that he works well with the others. One condition of membership is that everyone participates in a social activity. Our members belong to CDS, AMNLAE.[1] We're involved with health work, church activities, community education. Everyone of us is in the militia, and many have done service on the frontier.

And everyone agrees to this?

At first there was some objection to the militia requirement. But we explained that our cooperative cannot survive unless Nicaragua survives. Now everyone participates willingly.

Have you achieved the maximum membership?

We'd like to have more members. But we have serious problems. Right now our irrigation pump is broken. Unless we get the neces-

[1] AMNLAE—Luisa Amanda Espinosa. Association of Nicaraguan Women; Nicaragua's major women's organization.

sary part we're going to lose some of our crop. You see, there's a great deal more land available, but we can't handle it. If we had sufficient machinery and equipment, we could cultivate much more land. Then we'd welcome more members.

Tell me about the farm, about production.

We have title to 160 manzanas.[2] We grow a variety of vegetables: corn, beans, sorghum, soybeans, tomatoes, onions, cabbage, sweet pepper. This is very good land and we get three crops a year. On two of the crops we need no, or very little, irrigation. But the third crop, during the dry season, requires irrigation. There is plenty of water available, but we have to bring it up from under the ground. For that we need irrigation.

How are the members paid?

At the end of the year the secretary of finance goes over the books, and our surplus over expenses is divided among the members. In 1980, our first year, each received 25,000 cordobas. In 1981, 40,000 cordobas. In 1982 we had a bad year, so there was no income. We had to borrow from the bank. In 1983 each received 55,000 cordobas. This year, so far, looks very good. We should receive a great deal more. If we can get the pump working, it will be very, very good.

What about your debts, your obligations?

The banks have been very good to us during the first years. We've gotten credit for seed, fertilizer, equipment, and advances for our living expenses. We're up to date on repayment of loans. We're in good condition. We have a capital of 2 million cordobas in trucks, tractors, machinery.

You mentioned the secretary of finance. How is the cooperative organized?

We have three commissions: production, education, finance. The secretaries are elected by the members. I'm the secretary of education.

What does the secretary of education do?

First, of course, there is the matter of formal education—reading and writing and so on. That's my responsibility. Of our forty-eight members, only a handful could read and write before the Triumph.

[2] A common measurement of land in Nicaragua. One manzana equals 1.75 acres.

Now thirty-five can. The rest are learning. Last year five of our members completed their six years of elementary study. Now all of them are attending secondary school in Sebaco. They go to school at night.

Another important educational task regards discipline. Through education we encourage honesty and responsibility. That's political education. Before the Triumph everyone was for himself, for his own little family. Now we work to create respect for each other, for the community, for the nation.

Another task of the education commission is to avoid conflicts between the members. If some member is discontented or confused, we speak to him to avoid this misunderstanding.

The Education Commission is responsible for cultural activities—for our 14th of July anniversary fiesta, for instance. Sometimes we invite speakers from the FSLN. We show films. It's important work.

How would you describe the difference in the lives of your members before the Triumph and now?

All of our members were landless before the Triumph. They were poor, life was harsh. We were at the very bottom. I myself was a mechanic and a tractor driver on the farm of Juan Garcia. He owned 180 manzanas. Now, we have more than forty families living well on less land than this one man owned. I myself, I had seven children. At the end of this street is my house. I built it for my family. It's the only property I've ever owned. I had only two years of schooling. My formal and political education? I got it during the revolutionary struggle. What can I say? Before the Triumph we were always hungry. We were humiliated, degraded. We were the lowest of the low.

And the future? How do you see it?

Who can tell? The imperialists are trying very hard to destroy us. Our Nicaraguan counterrevolutionaries are desperate to turn the clock back, to go back to the old days. I mentioned the grenade attack last week. Last month two of our *compañeros* were assassinated. They were working in the fields and they were shot—dead. The counterrevolutionaries are trying to terrorize us. They want to destroy our cooperative, destroy all of the cooperatives. The imperialists are trying to destroy our economy. If we can't get parts for our pump and our other machinery, if they keep on killing us, who knows? It's possible that they could destroy us.

On the other hand, if we can survive, if we can beat back the imperialists and the counterrevolutionaries, the future is bright. I personally see the cooperative movement as the future. Perhaps the entire nation could evolve toward cooperatives. It could be very good.

But that's *my* idea. There are lots of other good ideas. We have to be able to try them, to see which suits the Nicaraguan people the best. This is a new country, and we can try anything, anything. The most important thing is to survive. If we can beat the enemy back . . .

———————— ◆ ————————

Maura Rayo, thirty-six, was the first woman member of the Leonel Valdivia Cooperative. She is a slender, fine-featured, handsome woman. Rayo wears a broad-brimmed straw hat while working in the fields. Her trousers are worn through at the knees. She works barefoot.

Maura Rayo

I was born in Chaquitillo. That's a small village just a few kilometers from here. In my family there were three girls, two boys. I myself have eight children. Some of the people joke about that. They say I'm very good at production.

My father owned a small piece of land—about five manzanas. But he lost that land. A man named Tirso Zeledon tricked him out of it. He stole my father's land and added it to his own. Zeledon owned a lot of land around here.

Then we all—the entire family—went to work for Tirso Zeledon. It was very painful. We worked on the very same land. Only now we worked for the man who had robbed us.

I was in the third grade at that time. I had learned to read and write, to add and subtract—nothing more. But they needed me to work on the land. So my parents took me out of school.

Here's an interesting thing. This very land that we're standing on—it is the land that Tirso Zeledon stole from us. After the Triumph of the Revolution the people took this land away from Tirso Zeledon and they started this cooperative. Interesting, isn't it?

I wish that my father and my mother were alive to see this. As a member of the Leonel Valdivia Cooperative, I got their land back for them.

I was married when I was seventeen years old. My husband worked for Zeledon, too. Life was very hard for us. We had no food. As simple as that. Most of the time we were hungry. We didn't know what meat was. Now there is plenty of food. Meat we eat two or three times a week, depending upon the supply. We get all of the vegetables we need from the farm, and what we buy, things like rice and cooking oil, they're not expensive.

My husband was one of the founders of the cooperative. I was very hurt when they wouldn't let women become members. They said that the work was too hard. Imagine, too hard for me, who raised eight children. When we worked for Zeledon I worked in the fields along-side my husband. I left the children at home and worked on my knees under the sun. I worked as well as any man. I think the real reason that they didn't accept us was that some men didn't want their wives working in the fields with other men. They were nervous, jealous.

My husband, Alonzo, was not that way. He fought to include women in the cooperative. Now he is very satisfied.

In the years before they permitted women I worked at home. I washed and ironed for other people to earn a few cordobas.

This is much better than working for others. It's hard work, but I'm accustomed to that. The important thing is that I'm a full member, the same as anyone else. I earn the same money as the men—as everyone. My children help me in the house. I have five in school, and my oldest daughter is in the seventh grade. Imagine, no one in my family or in Alonzo's family has ever gone that far in school. My daughter is smart; I think she'll go all the way.

I'm very busy, but in the evening, on Sunday, I do church work. I'm in the religious commission of our CDS. Another woman and I work together in this. You see, the priest rarely comes to Sebaco. We've asked him many times—we've offered to pay him. But he only comes when he wants to. The priest comes here four or five times a year. Some people say that he doesn't like us. I just don't know. So in our village we have a church but no priest. That's interesting, isn't it?

The other woman and I do religious work. If someone dies, we conduct the service. We do communion for the children, catechism. The only thing is we don't say mass. Also we don't marry people. So, many young men and women wait for the priest to come, or else they don't bother to get married. I like doing religious work. I've always tried to be a good Christian.

Since the Triumph of the Revolution, life has been good to my family. I'm contented, especially since now I'm a full member of the cooperative.

CIUDAD LEON, LEON

Eric Boone Diaz, twenty, is employed at the Silvio Mayorga Granja. The Granja is a state-owned hog farm several kilometers from the city of Leon. Boone is an assistant hog fattener. He is a husky young man— dark, handsome, curly-headed. He talks with confidence and seems a most mature young man.

I've been here at the Granja only six months. Before, I worked on a number of farms around here. We raised grains mostly—wheat and corn. I've always worked on farms and around animals. I like this kind of work. My father and most of my family always worked on farms, too.

I think I want to spend the rest of my life working in agriculture. That's why I'm going to study at the agricultural college. Right now I'm in my fifth year, my last year, of secondary school—I attend in the evening. But next year I'll start at the Nagarote Institute. That's a five-year agricultural program. The Nagarote prepares you to do any kind of work, in any type of agriculture. When I finish my studies there, I'll see.

Since the Triumph people like me, people from the countryside, have had much better opportunities. For instance, I am a worker *and* a student. Before, you couldn't do this. You were either a worker *or* a student. But now you can be both.

Now they do everything they can to help you get an education. For instance, here at Granja they give you time off to study. My books and my other materials, they're free.

I was in the military for four months. Only four months. One day my commander called me in. He said, "Eric, you're a good soldier, a good worker, a good student. You're a campesino, right? Do you want to go to agricultural college?"

Yucca farmer, near Masaya

I said, "Of course."

My commander said, "Go home. Get a job in agriculture. Continue your studies. Go to college. Nicaragua needs agricultural experts." Just like that.

So here I am. Now I work, study, work, study. I have little time for anything else. I like girls, parties, good times—things like that. But I have so little time. Who has the time for all of that?

What little free time I have I spend with the Juventud Sandinista. When I have a few hours I work with my compañeros. We paint signs on walls, buildings: "Sandino Lives," "Long Live the Revolution"— things like that.

For me, from every angle, the future looks good, very good.

———— ◆ ————

Responding to a question about the profitability of the Silvio May-orga Granja, Luis Reyes, the manager, replied:

Happily, we produce enough to meet our expenses plus a little surplus besides. But that isn't the reason for our existence. This is not a capitalist enterprise. We provide socially useful employment for forty-seven people. We also produce a socially useful product, pork. These are our primary considerations.

JUIGALPA, CHONTALES

Paul Bosh, thirty-five, is the general manager of Agropecuaria Canas Gordas, a very large rice farm near Juigalpa, Chontales. Mr. Bosh, nattily dressed in a plaid sport coat, seems more an aggressive, successful businessman than a traditional farmer. He is a well-spoken, confident, young man.

This Sandinista government has been very conservative regarding large privately owned farms such as ours. For instance, in the matter of loans they've been very cautious, very conservative.

Despite this, my family's rice farm has grown from 150 manzanas in 1979 to 1,000 manzanas today. We achieved this growth by buying more land every year. Yes, with loans from Sandinista banks.

It's a complicated situation. You see, this is a socialist government, and so naturally they prefer state farms, cooperative farms. Yet, they know that 50 percent of rice production in Nicaragua is from privately owned farms such as ours. So, in order to maintain rice production they have to make accommodations.

Most of the other 50 percent is from state farms. They used to be Somocista property, and the government took them over. There are very few rice cooperatives. You see, cooperatives tend to be labor intensive. Our industry, rice, is highly mechanized.

Rice production is up since the revolution. The yield is down, though. That is, we used to get around 80 quintales[3] from each manzana. Now the average nationwide is 70 quintales. But overall rice production has increased.

Nicaragua used to be a rice exporting nation, but not now. Now we consume all of our rice. That's because production in other areas, such as cattle, is down, and so our people eat more rice. Also, I'm told, the

3 A quintal is about 100 pounds.

people demand more food than before. So under the circumstances, where is it to come from if not from rice?

The price we get for our rice isn't bad. Listen, what farmer will ever say that he gets enough for his product? The rice is purchased by the state. They have a monopoly, and so they set the price.

But even under socialism, supply and demand influence price. They know that if the grower doesn't get his price, he wouldn't produce, so . . .

Another reason why so much rice is consumed is that the price to the consumers is artificially low. The state subsidizes the price of rice to consumers. Right now the subsidy is 15 percent less than the cost of production. The balance is paid for by the taxpayers.

The price of rice is revised upward every six months. That's not too often because of the inflation, the way things are going economically. Even then, sometimes the increases come too late, and then we lose money.

In other areas, things are not too bad. In the matter of insecticide and fertilizer, the government has been responsive. We have plenty, all we need.

But spare parts for our tractors are a problem, a serious problem. We use John Deeres, American tractors. But like all machines, they break down. You need to replace parts. If you need tires, hydraulic fluid, or even a battery, you have a problem. And there are hundreds and hundreds of parts to be replaced. We have to run around, make phone calls to the States, get the parts flown in. Believe me, it's a headache.

The situation with the shortage of dollars is very critical. There simply aren't enough dollars because our exports are down. And every capitalist government deals only in dollars.

Lately we've been buying more and more from the eastern European countries—the socialist countries. There are some Russian tractors available now. But for our purposes they're not as good. You see, in order to make two crops a year our machines have to work in two, three feet of mud, sometimes even clay. That's heavy pulling. The Russian machines aren't designed for conditions in the Nicaraguan rice industry. They say they're going to adapt them to our needs. That'll be good. I, for one, will be happy to use them if they do the job.

Also, the government recently allocated the rice growers $700,000 for parts for the next six months. That's very good. During the coming period it'll be very helpful to us.

There's a rumor that the Soviet Union is going to cut back on their sugar production and turn their sugar land into wheat. Then they'll buy their sugar from Nicaragua and Cuba. That would be very good. The Soviet Union is a big market, a strong market. Our sugar industry could provide us with enough currency to buy a lot of machinery from eastern Europe.

It's always hard to guess the future of our rice business. One thing is that the war is hurting us. That's a certainty.

Another thing for certain: We make it our business to stay out of politics. When businessmen today, private growers, get into politics, they get into trouble. So we of Agropeuraria Canas Gordas keep our thoughts on rice. We grow it as efficiently and as profitably as possible, and we have every intention of continuing to add to our landholdings and our profits.

LAS LOMAS, JINOTEGA

Eusebio Picado Gonzalez, forty-five, is a powerfully built, dark campesino. He has a thick, black mustache. As we talked, in time-honored country fashion, Picado whittled on a piece of wood. He is general coordinator of the Lina Herrera Cooperative.

Eusebio Picado

We have a good cooperative here. We have good land, even though the size varies with the season. You see, part of our land borders on Lake Apanas. That parcel is 200 manzanas—in the dry season. When the water rises, then its only 50 manzanas. That land on the lake, though—it's the best pasture, very productive.

Altogether, in the dry season we have 450 manzanas. On 80 manzanas we plant our crops. The rest is pasture.

We raise corn, tomatoes, carrots, beets, cabbage. This year we started potatoes. The government people came and made some tests on our land. They told us that this would be excellent land for potatoes. So we put in five manzanas for seed. Next season, if things go well, we'll plant a big crop of potatoes. There's a good market for potatoes in Nicaragua.

We get three crops a year of everything—even corn. There is plenty of rain around here, plenty of water during most of the year. During the dry season we use irrigation. We have a gravity system. It works very well.

The Lina Herrera Cooperative was established on November 26, 1979, by twenty-six members. That was only four months after the Triumph. Now we have seventy-eight people.

All of this land had been owned by officers in Somoza's army. After the Triumph it was simply lying here, unused. And we had nothing. We knew this land well. Before the revolution most of our members had worked on the farms that are now our cooperative.

After the Triumph people from the Agrarian Reform came to the village, and we all had a big meeting. They said, "Go ahead, take the land. Use it. Grow food for Nicaragua. But first, organize yourselves into a cooperative. We'll give you title to the land—free. We'll lend you money for seed, fertilizer, pesticide—whatever you need. We'll advance you money to live on until you sell your first crop."

Some of our people found this hard to believe. But others convinced them. We couldn't refuse an offer like this. What did we have to lose? We started this cooperative with one pair of oxen. That's just about all we owned among all of us.

It worked out for us. Now we don't owe anything above our obligation to the bank. After every crop we make an accounting and we divide the profits among the members. From the beginning we've made a good profit—every time. For our last three crops, each member earned 44,300 cordobas. In addition, each member takes as much of the vegetables as he wants. That's not too bad for campesinos, right?

Last October we bought this herd of 100 cows. They're Brown Swiss. They're good for both milk and beef. Thirty of our cows are milking now. Sixty-eight are heifers. We went to the National Bank for a loan for the cows, and they gave us the financing, just like that.

This herd was very important to us. You must understand, as a child I rarely saw milk—not me, not my father, not his father, going way back. Sometimes, once in a great while, there would be a bit of milk from a can, but never from a cow. We never saw fresh milk. For every campesino it was the same.

So now you know why this herd is important to us. Now our children drink milk. Every day. All they want. Every child drinks milk, fresh, warm from the cow. Our members buy the milk at cost—3 cordobas a liter. The surplus we sell to the community. Soon, as the herds grow, every child in Jinotega will be drinking all the fresh milk he wants.

As I said, we started with one yoke of oxen. Now we have seven. We do all of our work with the oxen. We own no machinery—not a tractor, not a truck, not even an automobile. It's hard working that way. We'd like to have at least a truck—we'd like to be fully mechanized. Maybe some day. But now I'm not so sure. When I hear other farmers talk of their problems with machines, with parts—I don't know. The oxen—we have unlimited pasture for them, unlimited water. And they never break down.

So far we've been fortunate here. We haven't been troubled by the counterrevolutionaries. Not yet, although we know that they're in the mountains nearby.

But we're prepared for the worst. We have a permanent *vigilanicia*. Everyone of us—all of our members—can handle a weapon. Forty-one of us are in the militia. We pray that we don't have to fight. We're farmers, not soldiers. Still, if we have to fight . . .

Our members are very active in social activities in the community. For instance, we've been working on a potable water system in the town. The Canadian people gave us $40,000 for this system. And the English, they've promised us a pump. This will be a big help. We've been working on this water system for a long time, and we hope to have it completed in five more months.

Also, we're working on a new school building right here on the cooperative. The government provided the material. We on the cooperative are providing the labor. You see, some of our members live here on the cooperative; others live in town. Everyone wants to live here, and so we're building homes for everyone, right here on our own land. When they're completed, when all of our people live here on the cooperative, the new school will be ready for our children.

Of my eight children, five are still at home. Two are in school. It will be good when our school is completed. We'll be able to use it for many things. Maybe in the evenings we can have adult education. Maybe we'll be able to have meetings. Maybe we'll show films.

It certainly is different from when I was a kid. I had two years of school. My wife, Esperanza, she had four years. We were both in the literacy campaign. Every one of our members was. When we began, only 5 percent of our people could really read and write. Now almost everyone can. Some difference, eh? Today the kids can go as far as they want. Even to the university. Who knows?

Look, before the Triumph I was a landowner. Don't be surprised. Yes, I owned *one* manzana. Every year I planted corn on my manzana. In addition, I was in partnership with other landowners. I grew corn on their land and I got half the profit—half the harvest. I had one manzana here, one-quarter manzana there, one-half manzana there—like that. I had no fertilizer, I had no pesticide, I had no irrigation. Most of the time I had no corn either. I did a lot of praying and we starved. Now it's a little different, eh?

———————— ◆ ————————

We have dumped lots of money—again and again—into small productive units that had never before had access to capital. They were not able to manage their resources efficiently, so instead of producing 40 units, they were producing 20 units. Somewhat romantically, at one point we were even traveling in helicopters and giving out credits to peasants who lived in very remote areas. The credits virtually fell into their hands from the helicopter. But who was going to gather the production? By which roads, by which means of transportation? Such romantic errors are made in every revolution. They are just the counter-productive side of the generosity of the revolutionists.
—Jaime Wheelock, Minister of Agriculture

SAN JUAN DE LA SIERRA, CARAZO

The land north of Diriamba, in the department of Carazo, is flat scrub. Even at the peak of this rainy season the vegetation is sparse, brown, thin. There are no lush, verdant fields of rice and sugar here. Here there are only ragged clusters of weed fighting their way through thin, stony soil.

The road to San Juan de la Sierra is rutted. Rainwater lies in the deeper pools, splashing the infrequent passing vehicles with sandy soil.

An occasional, sad-eyed bony cow stands staring in the road. Chickens peck and pigs root for their meager fare at the roadside. From time to time we pass lonely homesteads—unpainted hovels really. Hollow-eyed women and grubby children gaze impassively at the passing auto.

We stopped at the home of Octavio Baltodano. At thirty-seven, Baltodano is slight, work-worn, weary. A rusting bus languishes alongside the two-room stucco building. In the shade, beneath the vehicle, a large sow has burrowed a hole in the sand. She lies motionless, half-hidden from view.

Beyond the open door is a large main room, one of two in this house. At the rear of the room is a clay oven and a makeshift table. There are three or four stools and chairs. This rough, wooden furniture comprises the furnishings of the Baltodano home. A half dozen chickens wander about, pecking grit from the dirt floor.

Maria Baltodano stood by the oven, occasionally poking at the wood shards that serve as fuel. A pot of rice was cooking as she whispered softly to a toddler squirming in her arms. Other children sat on the floor alongside the wall, staring at the strangers.

Baltodano motioned us to a bench.

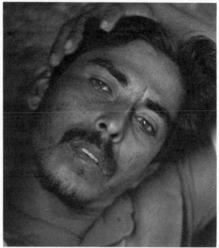

Octavio Baltidano

I was born in this house. It belonged to my father. I think that my grandfather built this place. I have five brothers and sisters, and they live around here, too. When my father died we made an arrangement. I got the house. They got other things.

When I married my wife eighteen years ago, she moved in with my family. She and I slept in the small room in the back, behind the curtain. At that time my parents were still alive, and some of my brothers and sisters lived here, too. We were crowded, but we managed. Now, only my wife and I and our eight children live here.

I have some land, a little more than three manzanas. It's not very good land, but we manage. It's out in the back, behind the house. I have no animal, no plow. So I pay a man to plow the land for me. We grow a little corn, a little sorghum. It's not much, but we manage.

My main interest, though, is my bus. You see that bus out by the side of the house? I used to carry passengers from San Juan to Diriamba. There's good money in transportation work. But for the past two months I haven't been working. I lost two tires. So the bus, it just sits there. I've been looking everywhere for tires. I've been to Diriamba, Masaya, Managua, everyplace. But I can't find any tires. There simply aren't any tires. So now I just sit here waiting, like my bus. I do a little farming. Most of what I grow we eat.

Food is a problem with us. We live mostly on corn, beans, tortillas. Sometimes there is an egg for the children. Did you see my sow? We never eat pork. I breed the sow and sell the baby pigs. Sometimes I trade a pig for beans, or I get a few cordobas to buy other things. Maybe once or twice a month we eat a piece of meat.

Sometimes we get a little bit of powdered milk for the children, but it's scarce. When I'm lucky and I get some milk, it goes in a day or two. So you see, my kids rarely drink milk.

Five of my kids go to school; the others are too young. This school here in San Juan only goes to the fourth grade, but my oldest boy is in the fifth. So he goes to school in San Gregon. The boy leaves here on Monday and he returns on Friday afternoon. In San Gregon he lives with a friend of mine. He works around the house and in the fields. In that way he earns his board.

I myself never went to school. My wife never went either. Neither of us can read or write. I could have gone to school when I was a boy, but I didn't. That's because my father was a butcher, and he needed me to help him in his work. So I didn't go to school.

A few years ago the literacy campaign came to San Juan de la Sierra. Many of the people learned to read and write then, but not me. In those days I was busy with my bus. I didn't have the time for school. Maybe some day the literacy campaign will return to San Juan. If it does, and if I'm not too busy with other things, I'll go. Maybe I'll learn to read, maybe I won't. It depends upon what I'm doing at the time.

I'll tell you something. I really don't like farming. I like driving the bus and carrying passengers. Look, I know two other men who have broken-down buses like mine. I'm thinking, maybe we could get together and buy one good bus. There's good money in carrying passengers.

LA TRINIDAD, CARAZO

La Trinidad is only a few miles from San Juan de la Sierra. Here, too, the poor, parched land shapes the life of the campesinos. Like San Juan, Trinidad seems to have been left behind. It, too, is the victim of insufficient rainfall, unproductive soil, years of crop failure. The people here, too, seem to be the unknowing victims of an "agricultural triage." They are the dispossessed of a poor nation with overwhelming needs and meager resources with which to meet them.

Alongside the unpaved road, beyond a rickety wooden fence, is a large wooden house. It is unpainted, rough, yet from the outside it seems quite orderly. An old woman sits in the shade in front of the house. She nods wordlessly to the visitors.

We walk past the house, down a steep, rutted path, to a shallow creek. A dozen stones are placed strategically across the creek to the far bank.

We cross this "bridge" and walk up another hill, at the top of which is a large field. Beyond, at the far side, is the wattle home—hut, really—of Marcos Mojica Aguilar, thirty-one years old. His wife, Maria Clorinda, watches suspiciously as Mojica greets us. A homemade broom leans against a fragile wall of the house. I watch as a parrot shuffles lethargically up and down the broom handle. Here, too, the familiar pigs, chickens, dogs wander freely in and around the tiny two-room house.

We are seated on rough stools under a huge shade tree in what might pass for the front yard.

I was born on this farm. My father owned sixty-five manzanas. That's a good bit of land, but not much when it's divided among twelve children.

I got this five manzanas when he died in 1981, and I built this house here for my family. Before that we lived in the big house near the road. Me and my wife and my five children live here.

Before my father died we lived with my father and my mother. Also two of my sisters and their families. That was a lot under one roof. My mother still lives there. Also one of my sisters and her six children.

This land here isn't too bad. It's level, and the river swings around right down the hill here, near our house. So we always have water for our needs. Even during the driest season the river is never totally dry. We can always get enough water at least to drink and cook with.

The problem with this region is that it's too dry for farming. This season has been unusually rainy. We've been lucky. Maybe we'll get a fair crop.

On my five manzanas I grow yucca, corn, watermelon, sorghum, carrots. Someone gave me some tomato seeds, and I have a good, thick bunch of plants coming up in the beds. So I'm going to plant a lot of tomatoes. On tomatoes, things like that, sometimes I can make three crops a year. Corn—I'll get two, depending on the rain.

Life for us in the country is difficult. It has always been so. My father had plenty of land, but with so many children, so many mouths to feed, how could he have anything? He worked hard all of his life and now he's dead. My mother is getting old, and I worry about her. She's been sick.

My father could never read or write—not till the day he died. I never went to school either, but during the literacy campaign I learned to read. So did my wife and my brothers and sisters. I don't read much now, though. Sometimes someone leaves a newspaper at my mother's house. When I see the newspaper I read it a little.

My children aren't in school. They're too young. My oldest, Marta Maria, is seven. She'll go to school next year. She should have started this year, but we kept her out. She had to help her mother in the house. So maybe next year she'll start to go to school. Maybe all of my children will go to school. Maybe they'll make something of themselves.

My kids have all been vaccinated for polio and other things. I don't know exactly which diseases, but I have the papers in the house somewhere. Would you like to see them?

Still, it is very hard for us. We eat meat two or three times a month, the same as before the Triumph. Whenever I can find a piece of meat I bring it home to my family. The children drink milk two or three times a week. I have a neighbor who owns a cow, and sometimes I get a little milk from him.

So you see, we have very little. The Triumph? Maybe now I'm perishing a little slower than before.

The problem with us farmers is that we're stupid. We lack intelligence. We live on the edge. We're not smart enough to fight for our needs. So we are the last ones anyone pays attention to. I hear about "the *revolution* this," "the *process* that." But really, I don't see any change. Maybe in Managua or somewhere else there have been improvements. But for us, here, nothing.

I like farming, but really it's too hard to make a living. I think about my life, about my father, and I don't know. I'd like to do something else.

I have a sister who lives in Managua. They're poor people, but somehow they seem to have more than we do. I visit my sister sometimes, and I see how they live. I think they live better than we do, and they don't work as hard. My wife has never been to Managua.

I think that next time I go I'll take her with me so that she can see for herself.

SAN JUANILLO, MATAGALPA

The road to the Carlos Galeano Gomez Cooperative was bad. In low gear we eased down rain-cut gullies. Slowly, we drove through stream beds—some dry, some not. We picked our way around boulders and over stones. There were barbed-wire gates to open and close and placid Brahmin and Brown Swiss cattle to nudge aside.

After eight or ten kilometers the road—path really—seemed to settle down. We passed a rude, one-room farm house and then another. Three women pointed the way to the field where the people were working.

We passed a cool grove of young plantain, then another house, and beyond it a large field of onions. Their short, thin stems were motionless in the still, summer air.

Two small boys playing in the road climbed aboard for a ride to the corn field. We passed a small, cool-looking church—its doors were open—and two more houses.

Then in the distance we heard the faint "chug" "chug" of a gasoline engine. It was the pump. Beyond a row of trampoline trees we spotted the thin spray of water irrigating the corn field.

As we drove toward the pump and the spray system, a young man, an insecticide spray can on his back, approached. Beyond him, at the far end of the field, were a dozen men working in the corn. Their machetes glinted in the sunlight.

The young man carrying the spray can was Julio Cesar Lopez, twenty-five, a slight, articulate, neatly dressed fellow. He was eager to tell us about himself and about the Carlos Galiano Gomez Cooperative, of which he is a member. We squatted in the shade of a tamarind tree.

Julio Cesar Lopez

This cooperative is twelve years old. It was established seven years before the Triumph of the Revolution. My father was one of the founders. *[The figures at the far end of the field grew a bit larger. The campesinos were slowly walking toward us.]*

At the beginning, twelve years ago, a group of campesinos joined together. They had no land, nothing. They had only their experience and the desire to work on land that belonged to them. So they joined together for that purpose.

All of the land around here was owned by wealthy people. Some of the land was being farmed. Other land, though, was just lying fallow. They thought that if they could rent some of this unsued land, they could build a good farm.

This land here was owned by a general in Somoza's army, a General Camilo Gonzalez, and it was not in production. So they went to Gonzalez, and they asked could they rent it. His answer: "I would prefer not to."

Then they went to the bank, which helped them to find other land. Now, this other land was also owned by a military man. It was not nearly as large or as good as this land, but he was willing to rent it to them—at 900 cordobas a manzana. That was a great deal of money in those days.

The bank advanced them 2,000 cordobas for each manzana, and almost half of that went to pay for the rental. The farmers had no machinery, no oxen, and so they had to hire other people to plow the land for them, also at exorbitant prices.

The other campesinos joined us. They ranged in age from fifteen to sixty years, and they squatted in a circle around us. They listened silently, gravely, nodding agreement from time to time.

They had little money for seed, fertilizer, insecticide, or food for their families until the harvest. But they worked very hard. Also, they were lucky. Somehow they produced a crop—corn mostly, and some vegetables. They paid their debt to the bank, they divided the few cordobas profit, and they borrowed for a second crop.

Now, the owner of the first farm, *this* farm, General Gonzalez, had a business failure—he went bankrupt. The bank took over the land. Then the bank went to the campesinos. The banker said, "Look, why rent that poor land at such high rates. We'll *sell* you the Gonzalez farm. It's a bigger farm with better land and more water, and it can be yours . . ."

Never mind that the bank charged 20, 25, 30 pecent interest. Never mind that one or two crop failures and they would lose everything. They had the opportunity to own their own land, something poor campesinos dreamed of but rarely achieved.

They abandoned the rented farm, and they established the cooperative right here. Now their lives were very difficult, because their obligation to the bank was very great. They did without. They sacrificed. They struggled. They dreamed that sometime in the future, they, or maybe their children, would own land. That was three years before the Triumph.

The rest you can guess. After the Triumph the cooperative was given title to this land. Free. The Agrarian Reform took the papers of indebtedness from the bank and destroyed them. Since then it has been a different world for us. We have a good life here with no landlord, no bank, nothing hanging over our heads.

We own a good deal of land here—475 manzanas. We get four crops of onions, four of tomatoes. We grow much garlic and corn. Our main problem is water—that is, the machinery to get to the water. If we could get better irrigation equipment, we could double our yield of corn. *[The silent, squatting onlookers nodded vigorous agreement.]*

You passed the cattle. We got that herd two years ago for the beef and for the milk. The bank advanced us the money for the herd and for wire for fences. That herd provides for our needs, but mostly we sell it on the market.

We also got credit for the plantain you passed on the road. We're trying out ten manzanas. If it grows well, we'll go into large-scale production of plantain. We've been assured that there's a good market for it.

We also got a loan for a tractor—a Bela Rus—with a disk plow. It's a Russian machine, and it's supposed to be very sturdy. We have another tractor, a John Deere. It was a good machine, but now it's fourteen years old, and it's in poor condition. *[One of the others interjected "Muerto—it's dead." The others smiled.]*

Of our thirty-four members, only six or seven have twelve years with the cooperative. Some have died or retired or gone elsewhere. Most of those who left did so during the earliest years when it was very, very hard. A few, like me, are sons of the founding members. Anyone can join, providing he is fifteen years old and is a farmer. It costs nothing to join our cooperative. The more people we have, the more we can produce.

We've made a good life here since the Triumph. We all took the literacy studies, and now almost everyone can read and write. There was a Cuban teacher in the village for a while. She taught the youngest children, but now she's gone. I don't know why. Maybe she'll return.

Nineteen of our members live here on the cooperative, and the rest in the village. When all of our homes are on our own land, it'll be very good. The farm will be safer. You see, so far we've been lucky that the counterrevolutionaries haven't bothered us. To tell the truth, Somoza left us alone, too. I think he was satisfied just to take our money in his bank. *[Another campesino interjected: "You came here on our road. The contras aren't crazy. They don't want to break their necks to get here." The others laughed.]*

We're prepared, though. We're all well-armed and trained. Look, life is good here. If not for the war, it would be perfect. If the imperialists would leave us to plant our crops . . . and . . . if we could get better equipment for irrigation . . .

CIUDAD LEON, LEON

Wilfredo Martinez Lazo is forty-seven years old. He lives in the city of Leon with his wife and three children. His attractive middle-class home is spacious and well-furnished, with an atrium and a garden. Martinez is a heavy-set man with a wry sense of humor.

Wilfredo Martinez

I suppose that I would be considered a medium-sized cotton grower. I'm not big enough to get rich, not small enough to starve. That makes me medium-sized, right?

I own 100 manzanas, and this year I'm renting 500 manzanas. Two years ago I rented 700 manzanas. Last year I rented 600. Every year a little less, see? Next year, who knows?

I used to be much, much bigger. I had a partner, Oscar Gallo, but he's gone now. Oscar's in Miami. They said he was a Somocista, and they took away his land and everything else. They gave it all to a cooperative.

Oscar had 1,500 manzanas. He had two cotton gins and nine airplanes. When they got finished with him, I was left with 100 manzanas. Not very much, right? But I still manage to make a living.

It's a struggle for me. My biggest problem is parts for the machinery. They're hard to get. Also, I have no airplane to spray my fields, so the government says that it'll assign one to me. That airplane—I'll believe when I see it.

As a private owner I have many other problems—problems with this government. They favor the cooperatives in every respect, so I always stand at the end of the line.

For example, take the matter of credit from the government banks. They give it to me a little at a time, so I never know if I'll have enough. This year, for example, for this crop they gave me 196 cordobas for each manzana. I've already spent 300 cordobas for seed, for fertilizer, and everything else. I have no idea how much they'll give me. I don't even know how much I'll need. I haven't even started to plant yet. The weather has been good, so tomorrow or the next day I'm going to begin.

Take labor. Things used to be much better before the Triumph. Now there's a terrible shortage of labor. Before there were always plenty of people looking for work. You had to send them away.

We used to get laborers from El Salvador and Honduras by the truckload. No more. They don't come now. I don't know why. I suppose it's because of the war. Here in Nicaragua there's a terrible shortage of labor. You can't operate like that. I think that there are too many men in the military. These soldiers—their labor is lost to us. So now we have to use machines.

Where we used to pick five-sevenths of the crop by hand and two-sevenths by machine, now it's reversed. That's the problem. Now we are more dependent upon machines. Understand?

In cotton, hand labor is much better. You get a better quality when cotton is picked by hand. Of course, the price you get for your cotton is better, too.

My future? Who knows? I don't know from one year to the next what I'm going to do. So I don't think about the future. In the meantime I continue to do the one thing I know well—grow cotton.

SEBACO, MATAGALPA

Ana Maria Lopez, twenty-seven, is a strong-featured, powerfully built woman with a great shock of thick, black hair. She smiles often and broadly, yet shyly. In the "old days," before the Triumph, she had been a prostitute. Now she is a member of the Leonel Valdivia Cooperative.

Ana Maria Lopez

I come from Jinotega city. My father was a campesino. My five brothers and sisters also worked on the land.

We were poor people, but no more so than many others I knew. For instance, we children had milk occasionally. Once or twice every week we had meat with our rice and beans.

When I was eleven years old I was finished with my schooling. Then I went to work as a maid in the houses of different people in Jinotega. Mostly I washed and ironed clothes, cleaned the houses, looked after the children. I did this kind of work for three years.

In those days I had some friends, maids like myself. We often talked about our lives, our work. We were children. We had nothing and we knew nothing. All we knew was work, work from morning till evening, every day of the week. We were all dissatisfied, and we talked about our unhappiness all the time.

Two of these girls, my friends, had become prostitutes. They worked in a house in Jinotega. They came to see us often, and they told us about this good life that they had. It was easy work, it was fun. They had pretty clothes, a lot of free time, things like that. They made it seem very attractive.

One day I went with them to that house. I became a prostitute. I was then fourteen years old. Now I know that those girls didn't think it was so good. The man they worked for made them go out and get girls like us. He paid them for that service.

At first I didn't mind it too much. I was fourteen. What did I know? Some of the men, the customers, were not so nice. But mostly they were pleasant enough. They were simple working men, campesinos. It was easy, it was quick.

We lived in that house—six, sometimes eight girls like me. We took our meals outside. The boss paid us half of all that we earned, and the rest he charged us for his commission and for rent. After paying for my food, clothing, rent, and everything else, I never had any money left over. But I didn't worry. I lived for the day. I was indifferent to the future.

Then later I began to think, what kind of life is this? Degenerate. Worse than an animal. But what could I do? Where could I go? My family? I couldn't face them. I was ashamed.

One time a man, a customer, came to me. He was a nice man. His name was Luis. He came back again and again, and he always asked for me. One day he said to me, "This is no life for a girl like you. Leave this house. Come with me. We'll get married."

I didn't have to think about it too much. He was a nice fellow. I liked him. So I left. One day I walked out of that house and I didn't return. I was then sixteen years old.

Luis was true to his word, and we got married. He was a truck driver and was good to me. But that was only in the beginning. Maybe, too, I wasn't such a good wife. I didn't know anything about keeping a house. Remember, I was still very young, and I had no mother, no sisters or friends to advise me.

The problem with Luis was that he drank too much. It became worse and worse. He never beat me or anything like that. But he began to abuse me, call me foul names. He would tell me how he had found me, how he had taken me out of that house, things like that. Then he did it more often, sometimes every day. I started to argue back, to fight with him.

It continued this way for a long time. Eventually, after we were together for three years, Luis started to see other women. Then he abandoned us. By then I had two children.

I had to feed my children. I had to support them. What could I do? Where could I go? I went back to that life. I became a prostitute again.

This new house where I went to work was owned by a Guardia officer. He was very strict. He insisted that the girls dress well. He bought our clothes for us and charged us double for them. Now I needed money to pay someone to look after my children. I was often short, and he insisted that I borrow from him. He charged us rates that you couldn't believe. We all owed him a great deal of money.

This Guardia officer used to point his gun at us. He said that any girl who owes him money and leaves the house will be a corpse. We were terrified. But now there was no way out.

It went on like this for four years, until the Triumph of the Revolution. My Guardia boss disappeared. They say he went to Honduras. Prostitution was outlawed and the house was shut down.

I was liberated—but for what? I had lived this life for many years, and I knew nothing else. Still, I started to do different things. I cleaned people's houses. I washed clothes. I worked in the fields. I did everything, anything, to earn cordobas for my little family.

One thing was very bad. People knew me. The women in Jinotega wouldn't talk to me. The men, many of them, wouldn't leave me alone. To them I was only a whore. On several occasions I was forced to have sex with men who kept after me. These were hard times for me.

Finally, I took my two children and I left Jinotega. We came to Matagalpa city. Here it was a little better. People didn't know me, didn't know what I had been. Once again I started to do any kind of work to feed my children and myself. Mostly I cleaned houses and worked in the fields.

I began to attend my barrio CDS meetings and I helped in AMNLAE. You see, I was very lonely. I didn't know anyone in Matagalpa, and in this way I made friends. Now I made no secret of my past. But people here didn't seem to mind so much.

One time I worked on tomatoes in the Leonel Valdivia Cooperative. They had a big harvest, and they hired people to help bring it in. I worked hard, but it was enjoyable. The people were good to me. They were friendly. They were fair.

After the harvest a boy came to my home. He told me that the cooperative executive committee wanted to talk to me. I had no idea what they would want to talk to me about, so I went with the boy.

The committee invited me to join the cooperative. Just like that. They told me that I had worked very well in the harvest and, as they had recently opened their membership to women, they were looking for some "high class" people. Imagine that! High class. Me! I accepted on the spot.

Later I learned that the AMNLAE people had spoken to the

cooperative executive committee and had asked them to consider me for membership.

These people here are more than only my fellow workers. They are my *compañeros*. They are my brothers, my sisters, my family. I belong here now as much as anyone else.

My children and I moved to the cooperative. We live in a room in the house of one of my *compañeras*. Soon, after the next harvest, when I have some money, I'm going to start to build a house here, a home for my children and me.

SANTO TOMAS, CHONTALES

Central Chontales, east of Lake Managua, is cattle country—beef and dairy. The three-hour drive in a government jeep is, for the most part, through valleys between steep, dusky mountains.

They tell me that this country was once heavily forested. Now, for the most part stripped of cover, the brown hills are in dramatic contrast to the green lowlands, the rich meadows seemingly locked in struggle for dominance with the thin desert vegetation of the higher altitudes.

Both in the lush lowlands and on the barren hillsides the cattle graze placidly in the Nicaraguan sunshine. Our jeep is frequently halted by the herds, prodded along the roads by boys and men on horseback. Perhaps, I speculate, they're searching for better fodder.

They say that the temperature, too, has changed. It is warmer now than in years past. Water tables have altered. Now there is desert where once there had been rich vegetation. The swamps and marshland, I'm told, are also newcomers to this land.

My companions on this trip are Melba Altamirano, of the Union of Farmers and Ranchers (UNAG), and Luis, an Argentinian. Luis came to Nicaragua to help with the literacy campaign, and he stayed on.

Santo Tomas, in central Chontales, is a sleepy country town 170 kilometers east of Managua. On this day, though, Santo Tomas is very much awake. It is the site of a meeting of Region Five of UNAG. The dusty street before the meeting hall in the town's center is jammed bumper to bumper with autos, jeeps, pickup trucks—the vehicles of the ranchers, the men whose lives are tied to these tortured hills, lush meadows, soggy marshes.

The building is squat, wooden, one story, and the banner above the door welcomes "Small and Medium Ranchers" to the meeting.

We enter. Perhaps 200 men and a handful of women are present. They sit silently for the most part, on folding chairs facing the front of the room. These are unmistakably ranchers, granderos. *Hard, weather-worn, all of them. Most sit with arms folded, silent, waiting, waiting. Wearing broad-brimmed sombreros and boots, they wait. Some of the younger men are engaged in earnest conversation. Their voices are hushed, their tones urgent. A number of gray-mustachioed old-timers, some with hands resting on canes, doze lightly in the cool room.*

This assemblage is in sharp contrast to others in the countryside, in the barrios. Ofttimes women predominate in number and spirit. Ofttimes the atmosphere is one of joviality, even carnival-like. Not here. There are no toddlers exploring the room and the unfamiliar faces. Even the ever-present curs have forsaken this convocation.

On the raised platform facing the audience are a dozen men and women. They are mostly young, and some are in uniform. These seem to be city people, representatives of UNAG, the Frente, the government.

A young man, black-bearded, rises and approaches the podium. Is he a representative of the government or of UNAG? I don't know. I missed the introduction. That he is not the Frente spokesman, I'm quite sure. I suppose that would be one of the uniformed ones.

The whispered conversations are hushed, and the ranchers, with arms still folded, learn forward in anticipation.

The young man speaks from notes, softly, earnestly.

Your organization, UNAG, the voice of Nicaraguan farmers and ranchers, is growing in number and influence across the nation. . . . Eight new organizations in other zones. . . . Here in Region Five we have strengthened our leadership. . . . more mature. . . . more experienced. . . . more effective. . . . purchasing cooperatives. . . . eliminate the middlemen. . . . less expensive feed, cement, spare parts. . . . beginning next month higher prices for our milk and cheese. . . . Beef production has increased 5 percent in the first six months of this year. . . . Milk production is up in the better areas. Where water is lacking, it is still below target. . . . upgrading our stock. . . . new breeding station. . . . importing fine Holsteins from Canada, Brahmins from Argentina. . . .

The audience listens impassively. Eyes narrowed, arms folded, they wait, wait. For what?

Fifteen, twenty minutes pass, and the black-bearded one thanks the audience for its attention. Amid polite applause he returns to his folding chair. Now a second speaker approaches the podium. She wears a neat uniform. A dozen words into her address, and I know that she *speaks for the Sandinistas. She is young, not more than twenty-three or twenty-four years old. Her dark brown hair is pulled tightly back on her head. She talks with passion, without notes.*

Compañeros, we're in a war. You are soldiers in the struggle for Nicaragua's survival. . . . food—your beef and milk are weapons. . . . The imperialists are forcing us to invest our meager resources in guns and bullets. The mercenaries are murdering our brothers and sisters on the frontiers. . . . Here in northern Contales they're burning our ranches, destroying livestock, attempting to kill our hopes and dreams. . . . The Yankee boycott hopes to strangle our economy. . . . *Compañeros,* brothers, Nicaraguans—we must survive, we must resist, we must produce. . . .

Once again, desultory applause. A minority, moved by her beauty, her obvious sincerity, her appeal to their manhood and patriotism, rise and shout their support.

Now the drama belongs to the audience. There are questions to be asked—and answered. One by one the grizzled ranchers, most with carefully chosen words, some with heat, rise and speak.

I need a road. The road to my *finca* has been washed out for two years and the bridge is impassable. In the rainy season I have no way to get in our out. Last year at our meeting, in this very room, I was promised . . . when will I have my road, my bridge?

There is scattered applause as he returns to his chair, muttering. Another rises.

It is impossible for me to remain in business. At the price the government now pays for beef, I can't stay in business. I may go out of business. I can't raise beef at these prices—not if I expect to stay in business—I lose money on every steer I sell.

Black with anger he plops into his chair. Another rises.

I have no wire. I can't get it. Not even for gold. How can a man be expected to raise cattle without barbed wire?

And another.

No cement. How can I increase my herd without new water troughs? How can I build troughs without cement?

I have two tractors and both of them just sit and rust. No spare parts. We were promised spare parts. . . .

And many more questions from the lean, steely-eyed ranchers. They are pragmatic, single-minded, demanding. Most are variations of questions previously asked.

No spare parts.
No wire.
Low prices.

Then, the response—this time by an older man, most likely the government representative—most likely, from his appearance, a farmer or a rancher. He is tall, lean, with a shock of gray hair.

Patiently, thoughtfully, he speaks. He offers hope; he predicts additional hardship and struggle. He speaks of the struggle against imperialism and the shortages of nails, wire, machine parts. He discusses the price of beef and Nicaragua's rejection by the International Monetary Fund. He invokes the brutality of Somoza, the venality of Reagan. He invokes the legacy of Sandino. He talks of international solidarity. He speaks of patriotism and treason, chauvinism and internationalism, the ugliness of the past and the hope for the future. He offers scant hope for today but immortality for those with the strength and the courage to persist.

Again, scattered applause. Again, whistling and cheers from the militant minority.

And then the meeting is adjourned.

On the adjoining patio a four-piece band—trumpet, violin, accordion, drum—explodes into a medley of folk and patriotic tunes. The bar is opened. Politics, the price of beef, shortages, the war be damned. The ranchers belly up for their rum and beer. Steaks, lean and tough as the men who produce them, are slapped onto huge charcoal grills.

A rancher, Geronimo Gonzalez, forty years old, reluctantly agrees to talk with me. Gonzalez is a big man—thick, broad through the shoulders, neck, and chest. His hands are mallets, his fingers, sausages. He is a dark man—heavy-eyed, with a great black mustache and a thick mop of ebony hair.

I myself, I started with nothing, nothing. I was eight years old when I said that someday I would be somebody, I would be a *grana-dero*. I started with the machete, and I worked and worked. Day and night. In the heat, in the rain, I worked, and I started to save my cordobas. One at a time. I worked when others my age played. I worked when they slept. They were eating, dancing, making love while I worked. One by one I put aside my cordobas, and fifteen years ago, when I was twenty-five years old, I bought my first piece of land. I payed in cash.

Then another piece of land. This time I got help from the bank. When you have something of value, you can always get help from the bank. When I was very young I learned that if you're nothing you *get* nothing.

Today I own two ranches. One is 2,000 manzanas, the other 500 manzanas. I own 500 head of cattle free and clear. So you see, I raised myself from nothing, nothing. Nobody ever helped me. I asked nothing of nobody. I did everything myself, and now I have troubles.

Oh, I make a living. My family eats. I pay my debts. But I have problems, troubles. I need nails, I can't get nails. I need wire, I can't get wire. I need machinery, I can't get machinery. The price of grain is too high. The price I get for my beef is too low. Understand?

For me there was no need for a revolution—for this Triumph. Nobody bothered me before. I lived good—better than now.

Then, without further ado, he pulls his bulk from the chair.

Adios. *Mucho gusto.*

Geronimo Gonzalez lumbers off in the direction of the crowded bar.

In contrast to Geronimo Gonzalez, Roger Gonzales (no relation) is dapper, almost delicate. Of medium height and build, he has reddish brown hair. Gonzalez wears a cap with a "Ford" logo, a white T-shirt, neat chino trousers. Roger Gonzalez is thirty-seven years old. He is married, with three children. He was anxious to tell his story to a foreign writer.

I'm a dairyman. I own a nice piece of land, 170 manzanas, sixty head of cattle. I got this land many years ago from my father. He owned a lot of land. This place of mine was virgin, unimproved. Eight years ago, even before the Triumph, I started to build a dairy.

It is very difficult for me, for all private owners today. Things have changed radically for them, for all of us, and it's not easy to understand. You must understand, too, that Nicaragua is an underdeveloped country. We don't produce well. We never did. We don't have the technical knowledge that we need. Our livestock is not the best.

Now, of course, there are shortages, yet the government expects us to produce, produce, produce. I can understand that. But we can't get the machinery and equipment we need in order to produce more. So it's frustrating. Nicaragua produces very little in the way of machinery, and we don't have the dollars to import them.

The government tries to help, but what can they do? They give us technical assistance, they provide credits. But it's never enough. And of course, what we desperately need—manufactured goods—we can't get at all. So it's frustrating. For the private ranchers and farmers it's very frustrating.

I can't make a living from my land. My wife is a schoolteacher, and without her income I don't think we could survive on the land.

What hurts me is the knowledge that I could make a living from my dairy *if* I could get better productivity. And to get better productivity I need better equipment and better cows. I know that the government is bringing in better stock from overseas to improve our herds. That's very good, but it'll be years until we see the difference.

If I could get better machinery, better livestock, then I could make a living—a good living. I'd buy more land. I dream of having a model dairy—a credit to myself, a credit to Nicaragua.

But as long as we suffer the aggression, things won't improve. First of all, there's the economic aggression from the United States. Then there's the military aggression. We have military aggressors right here in Nicaragua. That's the counterrevolutionaries. We have military aggressors in Honduras, in Costa Rica—wherever *your* country has influence.

And it's all such a waste. So futile. Because in the end the people of Nicaragua will win. Even these ranchers—the big ones. Some of them will never, can never, adapt to "the process"—to socialism. But most can and they will produce—because they're Nicaraguans and they want to work, to produce. The United States cannot hope to stop the advance of the Nicaraguan people. They can make us suffer—*that* they can do. But they cannot hope to stop the advance of our nation.

Ranchers, Santo Tomas, Chontales

Father and son, Jalapa, Neuva Segovia

EL VIEJO, CHINANDEGA

Sofie Izquierdo, twenty-six, is a tall, attractive brunette. She works at the Elisa Banana Plantation. Isquierdo is somewhat shy, reluctant to talk to a foreign stranger. As we converse, a child clings to her skirt. Another, a baby, sits on her lap. She is pregnant.

I live here in the little house by the main gate. That's convenient for me. You see, my job is at the gate. I'm secretary for *vigilancia* for the entire plantation.

There are sixteen of us working in *vigilancia*. We stop people and vehicles coming in and leaving the plantation. Everyone is armed, but if there are any problems that we feel we can't handle, we are supposed to call security. So far there haven't been any problems—not in the three years since I started to work here. But you never can tell.

Before I worked here I never had a job. My mother, she never worked outside of the house either—except maybe sometimes in the fields. With all of the women in our family it was the same.

I work seven days a week. That's a lot, but if I want a day off, all I have to do is ask. I've never been refused. I get my pay even when I take a day off.

The government—Elisa Plantation is owned by the government—pays me 600 cordobas a month. Also I'm given this house to live in. My three children live here with me. You can see that I'll soon have another. Also my aunt lives with me. And I have my *compañero*—Amador Villalobos. He lives here, too.

Amador works on the plantation. He's a foreman, and he earns 2,500 cordobas. Between us, with his earnings and mine, we manage pretty well. We have enough to eat. We pay no rent. If I need a dress or Amador needs a shirt or something, we can buy it. Also things for the children. We don't need much, and what we want we can usually get.

Amador and I have been together for five or six years. We're not married. No, I never think about getting married. To tell the truth, he's never asked me, and I've never thought to mention it to him. I'm content the way things are. I think Amador is, too. I'm going to ask him. Maybe I'll discuss this with him. We'll see.

One thing I think about sometimes is this: I had only two years of school. Now I think that I'd like to learn to read better. I'd like to know more about things—about Nicaragua, about the rest of the world, about many, many things. But it's not possible now. Not with three children and the new one coming. I expect the baby in four months. So how could I start school?

I was raised on a small farm in Chinandega. That's why I had so little education. My mother is dead, but my father still works with the machete. Sometimes he comes to visit me. He likes to play with the children.

I must admit that I'm not active in AMNLAE, CDS or anything like that. The reason is that no one has ever asked me to join. If someone asked me, I think I would. Yes, I believe that I'd like to be in AMNLAE or something like that. But in the meantime . . . I have my three children and my *compañero*. And now the baby is on the way. I'm content.

———— ♦ ————

In the dense, shaded groves of the Elisa Banana Plantation, eight men are working with machetes. They are trimming banana plants, clearing undergrowth. The men are soaked—not from perspiration, but from the rain of the previous evening, dripping now from the broad banana leaves. Their pace is relaxed and leisurely as they talk and joke among themselves.

Two of the men readily agree to talk to a stranger. The others light cigarettes, squat around us, and listen carefully. The two men are Pedro Gutierrez, forty-nine, a thirteen-year veteran of the plantation, and Agustino Navarro, fifty-two, employed at Elisa for ten years. The two have opinions on a variety of subjects.

Agustino Navarro

The cost of living

NAVARRO: It's much the same as before the Triumph of the Revolution. We get more money, but everything costs more, much more.

GUTIERREZ: These pants cost me 500 cordobas. A shirt like this used to cost 150 cordobas. Now it's 500 cordobas. Boots—they cost 1,000 cordobas. I work in my bare feet to save my boots.

Working conditions

NAVARRO: Conditions are better now. There's no doubt about that. In the old days they were very demanding. We all lived here on the plantation. In huts. At three o'clock in the morning they were after us: "Up, up, up." The foremen went around screaming. You really had to move. And here in the groves you really had to move. They shouted at us: "Faster, faster." Do you think that in the old days we could sit here like this, talking and smoking? Never.

GUTIERREZ: When there was no work they sent us home. Then we didn't get paid. Now we get paid whether there's work or not. They make a little job for you. Like we're doing today—clearing the underbrush, keeping the plantation clean. Sometimes we work on a trench for water pipes, or we repair the fences. You can always find something to do here.

NAVARRO: Bananas are perishable, very perishable. So when there is a ship coming in, we work very hard to cut the fruit and load it onto the trucks. At this moment there's no ship, so the bananas stay on the plants. So we're doing this little job. Nobody kills himself.

GUTIERREZ: One of the first benefits we got after the Triumph was about our tools. These machetes. We used to have to buy them ourselves. Now the company provides them. Also the company gives us a meal.

NAVARRO: They always fed us. One meal in the middle of the day. But in the old days it was rice and beans on a leaf. Now we get a little meat. And they give us something to drink. That's not bad, eh?

GUTIERREZ: Now our food comes on a plate. With a fork. They used to shovel the food at us like animals. On leaves. We had to eat with our fingers.

NAVARRO: One thing that's very bad. They make us work seven days a week. If you don't come on Sunday, they take two days pay from us.

That's unfair. It's very bad. We're getting our union to fight that practice.

The union

GUTIERREZ: Even before the Triumph we had a union at Elisa. But it was organized for us by the company. They used the union to control us better. Sometimes you couldn't tell the difference—which was the union, which was the company. After the Triumph we got rid of that union. It was no good. We organized our own union and affiliated with the CST. This is much better.

NAVARRO: The CST is better. But we have to fight for our rights—like working seven days a week. It's going to be a hard fight.

GUTIERREZ: It's going to be a hard fight. Everything's hard now because of the war, the blockade. The government is trying to pull the whole country up out of the dirt. It's a tricky situation.

Health care

NAVARRO: It's true that health care is free now, but there are no medicines. How can you cure sickness without medicine?

GUTIERREZ: I was sick. I had typhoid. So they took me to the hospital in Leon. In the old days, before the Triumph, who ever heard of a campesino from Chinandega being taken to the hospital in Leon?

NAVARRO: I had an accident on the plantation. And I also had a bad fever—I think I had typhoid too. So they took me to the hospital in Chinandega. That was a nice enough place, but my doctor didn't come to see me. Nobody paid any attention to me. I was dying. So I told my son to take me home to die. He took me to a private hospital and they cured me. The government paid for everything. So maybe it's good and bad, right?

GUTIERREZ: My grandchildren got all of their vaccinations free in the school. The nurse examines them all the time. No question about it. Health care is better now.

Education

GUTIERREZ: Although, Agustino and I had what? Four years of school? Five years? Both, combined. Today everyone goes to school. Even old people. I was in the literacy campaign. We all were. Now I read and write like a professor. Before the Triumph, the Nicaraguan people, especially campesinos like us, we lived in darkness. Now the whole world is open to us.

National problems

NAVARRO: The reason things are so expensive and scarce is not due to a lack of production. The government expects a war, and so we have to keep a reserve of everything. Food, clothing, machinery, everything. The government expects imperialist aggression on a large scale, so all of the young men will have to go and fight. See? No production then. There are people who don't like the government. They would welcome a Yankee invasion.

GUTIERREZ: Of course there are those against the government. But we know who they are. But the young people, the campesinos, they'll fight. The Yankees know that. If they invade us, we'll spill so much of their blood that they'll have to stop fighting. They'll go home. Also, the Yankees know that the Russians will help us. The Yankees don't want to fight the Russians. It could start a new war—all over the world.

NAVARRO: That's true. A war between the Yankees and the Russians. It could be the end of the world.

On the future

GUTIERREZ: I really don't think that the imperialists will invade Nicaragua. They're not that stupid.

NAVARRO: I wish I had such confidence. Our situation is dangerous, very dangerous.

SAN ISIDRO, MATAGALPA

Apolinario Gonzalez, thirty-six, is a tall, well-built attractive man. He chooses his words carefully, but speaks with authority and confidence.

I never owned land before the Triumph of The Revolution. My father owned nothing, nor did his father or any of my family. We were all landless campesinos. Maybe I'm the first one who has owned something.

Sometimes I used to plant a piece of land in partnership with the owner, or I'd rent one or two manzanas. But almost always I lost the

Apolinario and Melinda Gonzalez

crop—or most of the crop. I had too much rain, or not enough. I had bugs, disease, or the crop would just burn up in the field. Sometimes I would get a decent crop and then there was no market. Then I would hire myself out. I would work for other, rich farmers.

There are many rice farms in this area. I always preferred to work on rice. I like this crop. I consider it to be the king of crops. It's so neat, so clean. Look at the field. did you ever see such a beautiful green color? I liked it very much, but I knew that I could never own my own rice.

After the Triumph everything around here changed. We were told that we could own land now—but not as individuals. We were told that if we joined together in cooperatives, the Agrarian Reform would give us land. We were told that the government would help us with money and technical assistance and everything else that we needed.

Some others and I got together and we rented a private farm. We established a cooperative. People came from the Agrarian Reform and they helped us to write our regulations. We choose the name Mario Davilo Cooperative.

Then, two years later, this land became available. It is 170 manzanas. We—our cooperative—was given title to it. This land had belonged to a Somocista named Frederico Torres, but Torres hadn't used it for anything except for maybe a little grazing. It hadn't been planted to a crop. This was raw land, very rough.

We worked very hard. We cut the trees. We cut and burned the brush. We hired oxen to pull out the roots. We plowed this land. We had to break it up again and again. We ourselves dug the canals for water. We really had to work to turn this land into rice-producing land.

This farm is 170 manzanas, and we rent another 50. I'll tell you something: On this cooperative we get a yield of 120 quintales from each manzana. The maximum on other, private farms around San Isidro, is 80 quintales, and I know of some farms that get less than that, and they are satisfied. But we get 120 quintales. I think it's because we really push this land. And all of us, all of our twenty-two members, we have much experience in growing rice and other crops as well.

We have good equipment, and that helps. Yet we don't have all that we would like to have, or that we need. We have two good pumps for our water. We have one good tractor, but we need two more. Our tractor is a John Deere 3120—a good machine. We recently bought another tractor—a Bela Rus. We haven't used the Bela Rus yet, because it's in the shop being adapted for work in rice. We expect to have it any day now. Then, next year, we hope to get a third tractor.

We own no combine, so we rent one from a private owner. It's bad to have to rent farm equipment, because you can't have it when you want it. On the best days the owner, naturally, will use the machine himself. So we have to wait. We have it planned so that in two years we'll have our own combine.

This rice farming is very profitable, and our members do pretty well. We make two crops a year, and so we have an evaluation and distribution of our profits every six months. Last time each member got 18,000 cordobas. Before that it was 20,000 cordobas. Before that, 10,000. There's a very good crop in the field now. I expect that this one will come to between 18,000 and 20,000 for each of us.

Things have not always been so good. In the beginning it was very hard because we made very little money. I have a brother who was one of the original members. We lost a crop, and my brother had to leave. He has a big family, heavy obligations, and so he had to find other work to feed his children. He's been working as a *machetero* on private farms around here. Now I'm told that he wants to return to the cooperative. That's good. He's a fine fellow, a good worker.

I told you that in addition to our 170 manzanas, we rent 50 more. To tell you the truth, we'd really like to own that land. But do you know how much that 50 manzanas cost to buy? Fifteen thousand cordobas for each manzana! That's a lot of money, right? We'll see, I'm thinking that maybe when we have our tractors and combine all paid for, we'll be able to arrange something with the bank. We'll see. Maybe someday.

One reason why this is a good cooperative is that our members get on very well together. We do things together. For instance, we're all in the militia and in the military reserve. Also, we all live near to each other in San Isidro. None of us lives here on our own land. This land, it's too valuable for homes.

I look back over my life and I know that things are good for campesinos now. When the war is over it will be even better. The future? All you have to do is look around and you can see the future.

———————— ♦ ————————

Melinda Gonzalez, thirty-three, is the wife of Apolinario. Dark, trim, neatly dressed in a floral design blouse and white trousers, she is a truly handsome woman. In the presence of her husband and other male onlookers, she was quite reserved initially. As she continued to speak, however, she grew increasingly confident, animated, articulate.

My father was a campesino. He never owned anything—any land. I had two brothers and three sisters, and when I was very little my father moved out of our house.

We lived in San Isidro, and we were very poor. My mother—all of us—worked in the fields. Sometimes there was no work. Then there was no food. We had chickens, sometimes a pig or two, but we never ate chicken or pork. We sold the animals to buy our rice and beans.

Despite our difficult life, I was able to get five years of school. None of my brothers or sisters had as much. This education came in handy later.

When I was seventeen I married Apolinario. My marriage became my whole life. At first I could have no children, and I became frightened. I thought that I was barren. I feared for my marriage.

Then, four years after we were married, I became pregnant. I had a daughter. Then like that, I had three more. My oldest daughter is now eleven.

Life was hard for us. We never knew what would happen the next day. We never thought about the future—only today, maybe tomorrow. My children didn't know milk. Two or three times in a month

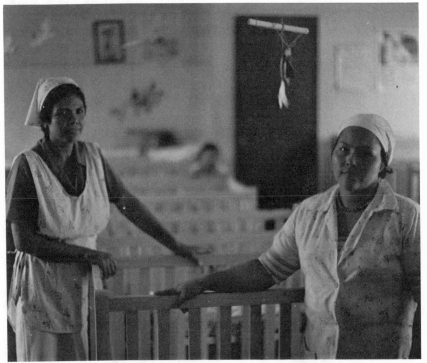

Nursery at the Chinandega Child Development Center

Old Miskito woman, Zelaya

they had a little meat. Sometimes Apolinario became very discouraged. I tried very hard to keep my family together. But what can you do? You have to go on living, right?

Then came the Triumph, and immediatly things changed for us. The cooperative, the farm—Apolinario told you about it, right? But for us other things changed as well.

For instance, before the Triumph we had no right to organize anything—not men, certainly not women. Now I myself belong to AMNLAE. If AMNLAE needs help for anything, I try to help. Sometimes we help a parent whose child has died. Sometimes we raise money for our boys fighting the frontier. But mostly, we try to help women with their problems.

In AMNLAE I do what I'm asked to do. I'm not on the directive board. The problem with being on the directive board is that you have to go to all of the meetings. I don't have time to go to all of the AMNLAE meetings. You see, I'm very busy.

You see, I work in accounting. I'm the cooperative's accountant now, and during the harvest, I must be here in the fields every day. My husband used to be secretary of finance. But he had to give it up because there's too much work in the fields. I used to help him with the books, and in that way I got experience. Also, I fell in love with this work.

This year the members asked me to take the job. I was very pleased. It's an honor, don't you think, to be entrusted with an important job? I get paid for this work. I became a member of the cooperative and I get the same share in our surplus as every other member. Exactly the same. No more, no less.

I didn't get special training. I learned as I helped my husband. Also, an accountant from the Agrarian Reform comes sometimes and he helps and teaches me accounting. So now I'm an accountant.

That's why I don't have too much time for AMNLAE or for other things that I would like to do. I'm lucky that my oldest is so responsible. Right now she's watching the other three. If she didn't look after them, I couldn't be here in the fields now.

It would be nice if we could have a *Centro Desarrollo Infantil*— [Child Development Center]—in San Isidro. Then I wouldn't have to worry about the children while I'm working. There are many other women like me who are working. It would be a help to all of us.

One time I visited a CDI in Esteli, and I liked it very much. I was really impressed with the way they treat the children. Something happened: I saw a child fall. He got a hard blow. They took the child to the hospital immediately. I liked that sense of responsibility.

Yes, I'd like for us to have a CDI in San Isidro. Maybe AMNLAE could take it on as a project. The problem is, who would take the responsibility to get it started? Everyone is so busy.

3
CITIES AND TOWNS

A Land of Country Villages

A mother is not simply a woman
Who gives birth to a child and cares for it.
To be a mother is to feel the pain
Of all children and all youth in our own flesh
As though they had all come from our own
    womb.
           —sign posted at the Francisco Dominguez
           Child Development Center in Chinandega

CASARES, CARAZO

Casares is a fishing village. It is also the seat of a farming community During "the season" it is a vacation area. Tourists from the cities of the north are drawn to its broad, white sand beaches and to the warm Pacific. Now, during the "off season" the village is quiet. Over a plate of warm turtle eggs, a local delicacy, I spoke with Oscar Mujica Parrales, a fisherman. Mujica is twenty-six, broad, a confident, ruddy-faced young man.

My family are not fishermen by tradition. My father is a farmer. His farm is about ten kilometers from here, on the road to La Trinidad. My four brothers and three sisters are still country people. They work on the land.

I started to come to the ocean when I was about eleven years old. I helped out around the boats. I cleaned the boats and the fish. I helped to mend nets. I ran errands for the fishermen. Sometimes they'd take me out with them. Then they'd give me a fish or two. That's how I learned about fishing.

I like fishing. I always did. What I like most about fishing is that you see your money every day. You don't have to wait, like in farming. A farmer never knows what he'd going to earn. It depends upon the weather, the market, blight—too many variables. And then you have to wait months for the harvest.

I have my own boat. That is, me and my two partners have our own boat. It's a good boat, twenty-four feet. We take it out a good way, although if it rains or if the winds are too strong we stay home. This ocean here, it can be dangerous.

We paid 5,000 cordobas for the boat and 15,000 for the engine. We got the money from our union—CUS. It was a loan.

The fishing around here is good. There are usually lots of fish. We catch mostly mackerel, red snapper, and shark. It's a fair living, but if we had a net we could do much better. Now, without a net, we take maybe thirty kilos of fish each day. With a net we could catch up to a hundred kilos. At 30 cordobas a kilo, that's not bad, right?

Our problem is that a net costs 3,000 cordobas. That's a lot of money. But now we're thinking maybe we can get a loan. We'll see.

There's good money in fishing. You see, there are three classes of fish. There's first class, second class, and third class. A man comes down here from Managua every day. He buys all of the first class fish. He sells them to hotels and the better restaurants in Managua. We get a good price for them. My share of the second and third class fish I keep. The woman I live with sells them from the house.

I work very hard. I have to work many hours. When I'm not actually fishing I'm looking for bait the next day. I have no time for recreation, except maybe sometimes I watch a baseball game. I used to like to play baseball, but now I'm just too busy. Who has the time?

I have very little time for anything but work. They want me to join the militia, but I don't have the time for that stuff. Also, I don't like it. I don't want any part of it. I'm a fisherman. I'm not a soldier.

I don't understand anything about political things, like the militia, the Sandinistas, that stuff. It doesn't interest me. Political things are not a part of my life.

You see, I don't read or write. I never learned about those things, and I don't care to. There used to be a literacy campaign in Casares, but I didn't go. I just didn't care to. I found that for my work I don't have to read, I don't have to write. I just have to be a smart fisherman, and you don't learn that in books.

I don't bother to vote in elections. How could I vote? I don't know anything about political matters.

My major interest is my work. If I could get better equipment, I'll be a better fisherman. Right now, a net would be perfect for me.

———— ◆ ————

On the next street from the restaurant in which I talked with Oscar Mujica, is the hotel-restaurant Casa Mar. This establishment is owned and managed by Eneas Guido Jiron. Guido Jiron, a stocky, energetic man of forty-two, is also the general coordinator of the Casares CDS. Without hesitation, he expressed pleasure at the opportunity to answer questions posed by a foreign writer.

I must apologize for the hotel's appearance. We just had Holy Week, the busiest time of the year. Now we have to clean up, paint. We have a lot of repair work to do.

Did you have a successful season?
Oh, yes. There's a lot of money around now. More people working than ever before. So we get a lot of people from Managua, from Masaya, from Grenada, even from Leon. We were totally occupied. I don't think that there was an empty room in Casares.

How many people live in Casares? How many are in the CDS?
In the town itself, there are 925 people. Mostly, they're fisherman and farmers. We have 200 CDS members. That's not including people who belong to other popular organizations.

What organizations?
We have the women's organization, AMNLAE, the ATC—that's the Association of Workers and Farmers. Also, there's the Fishermen's Cooperative, and other organizations, too.

What does the CDS do in Casares?
We're involved with everything that affects the welfare of the community. We watch prices to prevent unfair gouging by some of the merchants. Also, if someone gets into trouble or goes to jail, we look into it. We investigate to make certain that justice has been done. There have been cases when we got people released when the circumstances warranted it. If there is a national promotion to raise funds, we participate. We work in the vaccination campaigns—we go door to door. We see to it that our coast is kept clean especially during the tourist season. We assist in education. We see to it that every child gets fair treatment. Everything that affects the welfare of the community is our business.

The children seem to be active and healthy.
Exactly. We have many more children going to school than ever before. Illiteracy is a symptom of social and economic oppression. In not too many years it will be gone.

CDS office, Esteli

And health care?

Malaria used to be a problem in our region. Now the Ministry of Health fumigates for malaria. We go from house to house. So malaria is disappearing. This is an integral part of our process.

I've spoken with campesinos in this area—in San Juan de la Sierra and in La Trinidad. Just a few minutes ago right here in Casares I talked with a fisherman. They didn't express approval of the process or of the government. As a matter of fact, they were asocial, if not altogether antisocial.

I'm aware of people's attitudes. We have frequent meetings about the government's plans and programs. We make no secrets of the government's problems, even of its mistakes. These meetings are open to everyone. But many of the people don't participate, especially some of the fisherman. We worry about this. We would like them to participate. We encourage them to voice their opinions. We are very easygoing. We try to be nonpolitical, to put people at their ease. Nevertheless, many people don't participate. Their social structures are fixed, especially some of the fishermen.

Do you worry that some of these people may be influenced by counterrevolutionary ideas and activity?

Very much so. Look, during the revolution Somoza kept screaming "Atheistic Communism is coming. If I am defeated the godless Communists will take over." Now, the Sandinistas are victorious, and for many the logical conclusion is "The godless Communists have taken over." You see, mindless anti-Communism did not end with the Triumph of the Revolution. The opposition keeps these lies, these fears, very much alive. Sometimes we go to people's homes to discuss say, health care, education, or other social programs. They slam the doors in our faces. They say, "We don't talk to Communists."

Sometimes there is a lot of rough talk. Look, people are strange. I'll give you an example. This area around here is beautiful. Rich people have always owned homes here, near the sea. There was a man, Adolfo Calero Portocarero, who had a vacation home, an estate here. This man was the head of Coca-Cola in Nicaragua, a millionaire many times over. He was strongly, actively, against the process. After the Triumph of the Revolution, like others of his kind, he ran to Miami. So we took over his estate. We turned it into a fine hotel. Now this property belongs to the people; it adds to the wealth of the people of Nicaragua. Now what do you think? Many people are resentful that we took this property from that guy—that the state, the people—expropriated it. Not only the rich ones. Poor people, as well.

Can you believe it? It's true. That is the reality. It's not how we wish things would be. But it's the reality of life here in Casares, in Nicaragua. This is what we have to deal with. The reality. But we are patient. We explain over and over again—patiently. Meanwhile, we go on with our projects that will benefit the people, the community, the nation. Hopefully, during the course of time and their experiences, they'll learn. If not now, maybe later.

What projects?

Right now we have two important ones, both in the early stages of construction. The first is a new potable water system. Drinking water has always been a problem here. The other is a building project for forty-two homes for poor people, mostly for fishermen and farmers.

You believe that these projects will win more support for the revolution?

Certainly. Our CDS in Casares is growing, both in the number of our members and in the militancy of our members. Look, with all of the arms at our disposal, our main mission is to defend the revolution. This is not only a matter of weapons. We defend the revolution by performance and persuasion. The people who do not participate, who are confused, we don't try force to change their thinking. We explain, explain, explain. Many times we have to tolerate rough words, rough treatment. But we are patient. We have only one goal: to defend the revolution, to expand "the process." We must be patient.

CIUDAD LEON, LEON

Marta Medina is of medium height, attractive, thin, intense. She is twenty-nine years old, a physician.

I come from a large family. There are eleven of us, eleven sons and daughters. We were not poor people. We didn't suffer hunger, disease, exploitation, like so many others did under Somoza's dictatorship.

My father is an accountant. He's still working. My mother was a primary school teacher. She's retired now. Most of my brothers and sisters are professionals—doctors, lawyers, and so on. I'm a physician. I'm a graduate of the National University in Leon.

All of us, with maybe the exception of my father, are committed to the revolution, to the process. My father, he's conservative. But he respects our beliefs. We've always been a close family. There had always been much love in our house, and I think that with that attitude many differences, in politics as well as other things, can be overlooked, even respected.

At the time of the Triumph I was twenty-four years old, a woman. I was not a militant or even active in the insurrection, but I understood what was happening. I was very much aware of the injustice in Nicaragua under the Somoza dictatorship.

I think I began to be aware when I was fourteen, fifteen years old. I attended Catholic school. You see, I come from a very religious background. We, my family, we're devoted Catholics. And so, even as a child I was very much aware of the poverty and injustice in Nicaragua.

With the Triumph of the Revolution I became committed to the reconstruction and transformation of my country. And it's the best thing I ever did. It has become the center of my life, because I'm constantly growing. I'm a better person than I was last week, last year. Now my life would have no meaning if I was not in the struggle.

Right now, at this minute, I'm on vacation. You see, I attend school in the United States. I'm studying Public Health at Johns Hopkins University, in Baltimore. I'm not too happy there, but it's something I have to do for my country, for myself. I'm not happy, I'm not comfortable in Baltimore. I'm uncomfortable with North Americans. I don't understand their values, I don't like their way of life. But—I'm getting a good education.

Maybe it seems strange that I attend a university in an imperialist nation to be more effective in the struggle against imperialism? But why not? We have students in the Soviet Union, in Cuba, in the United States—in all of the advanced nations. We'll take the best from each to construct a new, socialist Nicaragua. That makes good sense, right?

OCOTAL, NUEVO SEGOVIA

Modesta Martinez, thirty-six, weights perhaps 105 pounds. She is small, dark, and hard as hickory. Her raven hair is pulled tightly back, revealing a high forehead and a fine-featured, brown face.

Having passed several nights in the home of Modesta's family, I know them and their routine well.

Modesta Martinez, left, and family

They live in a windowless, two-room mud house on the side of a steep hill in the barrio Jose Santos Rodriguez. There is no electricity— a kerosene lantern provides light. There is a crude, clean outhouse "out back." Water for cooking and washing is drawn from the river 150 feet below the house. The path to the river is rocky, steep, rutted.

The main, sleeping, room contains a half-dozen cots and hammocks. The floor is hard-packed dirt. On a rough wall of the main room are two colorful posters—one of the Pope, the other proclaiming solidarity with the people of Guatemala.

In the back room, the kitchen, is a large clay beehive oven, fueled by wood. The furnishings are sparse, almost nonexistent—a small table, three or four rough chairs and stools. Our conversation took place at the Ocotal Child Development Center, Modesta Martinez's place of employment.

I was born in Ocotal, in the very same house I live in now. The house belongs to my mother. She lives with me. My son, Noel, lives with me.

He's eleven years old. Also my sister and her two children. Another boy, Martino, lives in our house. He's thirteen, and he has no family, no place else to live. We're accustomed to tight living, but there's always room for a cot for one more, right?

My father, he was no good. He had many women and he wasn't home very much. He was a big drinker, too. He didn't work very much, but when he did work, it was in the woods, in the sawmills. My father died sixteen years ago.

We had two girls and five boys in my family, and we all lived together in our little *ranchito*. So you see, we're accustomed to being crowded. Most people in our barrio live tight like we do.

When I was growing up we had no electricity, no water—we still don't. We draw our water from the river at the bottom of the hill. For light we have a kerosene lantern. For cooking we use wood. Sometimes, when we can get it, we burn charcoal. That makes a good, hot fire. But charcoal is scarce, and it's expensive. So most of the time we use wood.

I had one year of school, and then my mother took me out because she needed me at home. I worked in the house with my mother. Then I began to clean other people's houses. In that way I made a few cordobas to bring home to my family.

I've been cleaning other people's houses all of my life. I don't mind the work. Someone has to do it. I never earned much money, but the little bit I earned has always helped.

Now I do the cleaning at the *Centro Desarrollo Infantil*. I like it here very much. I've been at the CDI for six months, and I think it's the best job I ever had.

Isn't this a beautiful place? The gardens—oh! This used to be a private home—for one family. It belonged to rich people. At the time of the Triumph they left Ocotal. Maybe they left Nicaragua. I think they thought that we were going to kill them [she laughs].

So now we have this house for the children. I love working here. Aren't the children beautiful? For me it's a pleasure to be here—to listen to them singing, laughing.

Since the Triumph of the Revolution life has changed for me. It's still hard, but at least we no longer know hunger.

Last year I was the CDS leader in my barrio, San Jose Rodriguez. That's 3,000 people in my barrio. Can you imagine me, with only one year of school, with such a responsibility?

In our barrio we have a health brigade. We learn first aid, we clean up places that breed sickness, we learn about the proper things to eat.

The aim, you see, is to prevent sickness, so that we don't get sick, don't have to see the doctor.

As the leader of our CDS I helped to organize a volunteer brigade to pick coffee on the boarder. Honduras is right over the mountains, you know, and it's dangerous for us there. But the coffee, the coffee crop, is very important to our economy, and so we volunteer to pick it.

Our CDS, it organizes men and women to keep the streets fixed. We do many things like that. Everything we do is important because we don't have any money, and the people must do these things themselves. In this way we work for ourselves and for the barrio. That's why our CDS is so important.

Our CDS also organized our health care program. Very important. I myself took a course in preventative medicine.

Now when we get sick we go to the new health center. It only costs us 10 cordobas. That's nothing, just a fee. The medicine is free, but sometimes there isn't any medicine. Before the Triumph there was plenty of medicine, but no one, no poor people, could afford it. Now,

AMNLAE Fundraiser, Esteli

medicine is free for us, but it's scarce. That's because of the war. All of our money goes into the defense against aggression, so there is nothing left for medicine. Most of the medicine that we get now is given to us by friendly countries.

But even so, it's better now. Before, when we were sick we had to pay a lot of money to see a doctor. Before, if you had no money, you could die for all anyone cared.

Our health care center is a long way from Barrio Jose Santos Rodriguez. We need a new one right in our own barrio. But I don't know. It doesn't look too likely as long as the war continues. But we keep agitating anyway. You have to agitate. You have to fight for what you need, or else you never get anything, right?

I'm active in my church, Iglesia San Jose. I'm on the parish council. The nuns there are North Americans. They've been very good to us, especially Sister Maria. She's a trained nurse, you know.

Life is better for us now. But it's still difficult. Every day the counterrevolutionaries are murdering our people. They are trying to destroy our economy. These people are beasts. They have no respect— not for old people, not for women, not for babies. All that those people know is killing, destroying.

Those counterrevolutionaries are Nicaraguans. But they don't look upon us as brothers and sisters. They receive pay from Reagan. That's why they want to destroy our country. That's why they kill us. Does your President Reagan have no heart? Doesn't he know that he's giving weapons to animals who have no feelings?

They say that we're Communists. Reagan says that. The rich people here in Nicaragua also say that we're Communists. Are we Communists? I don't know. We're Catholics. I know that. Can Catholics be Communists, too? I don't know. I have to think about that.

Look, I don't think that Communists are bad people. The Communists help Nicaragua. Fidel Castro, he's a Communist, and he is a friend to us. This gives me much to think about. I really don't think that Communists are bad people. Meanwhile, I'm very busy. I do *vigilancia*. At night I patrol. I carry a gun. I'm trained to use it and I'm a pretty good shot.

Would I use my gun? Look, I never thought that I could kill another human being. But I'm ready. If the contras come here, if anyone comes here, I'll kill. I'm ready to kill to defend my country.

———— ◆ ————

Joan Uhlen, a Maryknoll nun, invited me to accompany her to the weekly meeting of the Barrio Sandino Artesenia Cooperativa.

A group of perhaps fifteen women in this poor Ocotal barrio had established the cooperative to produce handicrafts for the tourist industry. They make blouses, bark bookmarks, wall hangings, necklaces of seeds and shell, and other trinkets. As a cooperative they purchase their materials in quantity, they discuss designs, marketing, and all of the other details necessary for the success of their small business.

During the course of the meeting, held on the porch of the local CDS headquarters, I noted that much of the spark, the leadership, was provided by Lulu Gonzalez, a vivacious woman in her mid-twenties. She led and directed every aspect of the business at hand—designs, expenses, prices, etc. Obviously a capable person, she easily commanded the respect of the others, some many years her senior.

Later Joan visited Lulu's home to see a shipment of newly arrived fabrics. I tagged along, intrigued, anxious to know something more of this interesting young woman.

Do you have children?
Yes, three.

Do you make crafts full-time?
Yes, it's my living.

And your husband? What does he do?
He's a worker on a farm—but he's not here. He's in another home. [Her face darkened, and the story was told. I dropped the discussion.]

Later, Joan told me, "It's a shame about Lulu. Her husband left her. He moved in with another woman. He took her refrigerator and just about everything else of value—everything she owned." I was surprised.

Didn't the CDS or anyone do anything about it?
In this country the men still have it pretty much their own way. They come and go and do just about anything they want.

But the law?
In order for the law to work, Lulu has to file charges against him. But she won't. He comes around from time to time—sometimes with a few cordobas for the children, more often to beat her. He bangs her around something fierce—bruises from head to foot. He says that if

Street scene, Granada

she complains, if she files charges against him, he'll kill her. And she believes him. I don't know what to do about it. Do you?

LA PAZ CENTRO, LEON

Clementina Mederano, forty-two years old, is an artisan. She lives with her husband and three of her five children in a small, rude house off the main street of La Paz Centro.

I work in clay here in my home. You can see that the biggest room in my house, the lightest room, is used for my work. My work is important to my family. For many years it has helped to feed us.

I make little pigs, toys, plates, ashtrays. I do the entire process myself. I start with raw clay and go all the way to the finished product. I sell my clay pieces to a dealer. He sells to vendors in the markets in Managua and other places.

This work isn't bad, but to tell the truth it doesn't pay me anymore. The cost of everything is too high. Clay, firewood, paints—they're all too expensive. It just doesn't pay me.

Everything today is too expensive. Meat is very high, very high—when you can get it. The same with cooking oil. Cheese, chicken—you can't touch it. Things are very difficult for me now.

To tell the truth, the Triumph has done nothing positive for me. What little I have I spend to feed my children. My two oldest daughters are married and out of the house. The three youngest are home with me. Two are in school, the other is still too young.

My husband and I don't do much of anything. He works for Telcor—the telephone company. But both of us just work, work, work. Everything that we do is to provide for our family. We have absolutely no recreation.

I belong to AMNLAE, the women's association. But it doesn't do much. We have meetings, sometimes we have a sale or a fund-raiser, although I don't know what becomes of the money that we raise.

The CDS? In La Paz Centro we haven't had a meeting in three months. I think that the CDS is dissolved here. At our last meeting a woman came in. She was drunk. She screamed at the coordinator. This woman said that her three sons were in the military—that it was his, the coordinator's, fault. She said that he put them there, that he took them away from her to die on the frontier. It was a big argument. She screamed plenty loud. At that meeting there were other fights and arguments, too.

So now I think our CDS head is afraid to go on the streets in La Paz Centro. I think he's afraid to meet the people.

We're trying to get a new coordinator here. I think we need one.

GRANADA

While walking along a street in the old colonial city of Granada I came across a storefront with a large painted sign that said "Obrero Club Social"—Workers' Social Club.

I entered the room. It was barely large enough to accommodate three ancient, scuffed pool tables. Two young men shooting pool nodded in my direction. They were in their early twenties.

The walls of the room grabbed my attention. They were blanketed with photos, banners, posters of Nicaraguan revolutionary heroes—Sandino, Fonseca, local martyrs. There were clippings from Barricada *and* Nuevo Diario.

The proprietor, Fernando, was a genial middle-aged man. He casually agreed to my request to photograph the room and the pool players. I did so, all the time trading quips, friendly insults, and idle chatter with the young men.

Then I asked Luis, "Are you a Sandinista?

"Todo"—totally.

"And your friend?"

Xavier preferred to speak for himself. "Cien por cento"—100 percent.

"Why are you a Sandinista?"

"Because I'm a Nicaraguan and a worker. With this last word, Xavier's eyes darted to the open doorway. I turned quickly as a dark young beauty floated by. Xavier shuddered. "Ai Dios, que linda!""—Oh, my God—how beautiful!

Xavier

CORINTO, CHINANDEGA

Juan Jose Urrutia Gadea is a longshoreman. He is twenty-nine, although he seems younger. Urrutia is very friendly and candid with a foreign stranger. He is slightly built, although muscular, and light-skinned, neatly dressed.

Right now, at this moment, things are going well for me. There is much work. During the mining of the harbor things were very bad, though. There were few ships coming in. No work. Some weeks I earned 500 cordobas. With 500 cordobas today you can buy nothing in Nicaragua. Nothing.

But now it's different. Last week I worked fourteen eight-hour shifts. That's right. I worked around the clock. Last week I earned almost 2,000 cordobas.

Ships of many nationalities are loading and unloading cargoes in Corinto now. Mostly it's Russian and Cuban, although during the last month I've worked on Japanese, North Korean, Spanish, Panamanian, and others.

Last week, though, it was all Russian. I loaded three ships with sugar, sesame, and cotton. I unloaded one big Russian ship. She carried 286 automobiles—Ladas. She also had a lot of dry milk.

Mostly, we unload wheat, corn, general merchandize, machinery, fertilizers, and milk. We ship coffee, cotton, sugar, sesame, bananas. For me, though, it's all the same. One cargo is the same as another.

So last week I was a very busy man. Two thousand cordobas, though, really isn't a lot of money. Not today—not the way everything costs so much.

I'm the head of a family. I support my two children, my mother, my two sisters. My mother lives on a small farm near Monte Rosa, and I send her money every week for the children and for my sisters. My boy is seven, my girl is three years old.

Actually, I have three children. My first *compañera,* when we separated, she took our little girl with her. This last one, though, she left the children with me. That's good. My mother will raise them properly. They'll get an education.

My *compañera* left me two months ago. She simply found another man who she preferred, and she went with him. I have no hard feelings. I'm not angry or anything like that. Listen, she came to me freely, and she was free to leave if she wished. That's her right. I'm just glad that she left the children with me. They'll get an education. Better than I got.

I have no education. I can't read or write. Nothing. I didn't have even one day of school. You see, I grew up in the country. When I was very little my father deserted us. I was raised by my mother. By the time I was eight years old I worked from four in the morning to four in the afternoon. For this I was paid 2 cordobas. I worked with the machete for eight years. Who thought about school in those days?

When I was sixteen I came to Corinto and I started to work on the docks. I've been here ever since, for thirteen years. But I've never lost touch with my mother, my family. I've always sent her something every week, regardless of how little I earned.

When the literacy campaign came to Corinto I started to learn with them. But I couldn't keep it up. You see, on the docks sometimes we work days, sometimes we work nights. You never know. When a ship comes in you work, regardless of the hour. So I couldn't keep it up. It was the same with the militia. I joined the militia, but I couldn't keep up with the training because of my work.

The mining of the port was very bad. It was very bad for the people, very bad for Nicaragua. Without imports our country can go down very fast. It's the same with exports. We must sell our products in order to survive.

Look, I know why they mined the water. The imperialists are making the war in order to take away the few privileges that we've gained since the Triumph. They want to take over Nicaragua again. They know that although we are a small country a lot of money can be made in Nicaragua. They want that money. Our Sandinista government, though, it wants to use that money for the people. It's really very simple, isn't it?

JALAPA, NUEVA SEGOVIA

While walking along a side street in Jalapa I came across an old, one-storey, brick building, sporting a new sign above the open door "Biblioteca"—Library.

I entered. In this one-room library were six sturdy wooden tables with new wooden chairs neatly arranged around them. My attention, though, was taken by what seemed to be acres of empty shelves lining the walls. There were neatly arranged sections: History, Biography, Novels, etc. There were twelve books in this section, eight in that, fourteen in that one, and so on. All of the shelves together, it seemed to me, contained a total of less than a hundred volumes.

The librarian, seated at her desk, was a very young, very attractive woman of perhaps twenty years. I learned later that she was lame—she walked with a severe limp. Her name was Maria, and perhaps she took note of my shocked surprise at the paucity of reading material in this library.

Maria

Our new library. The first ever in Jalapa. It's not much yet, but you come back next year, and you'll see all of the books that we have. Imagine [she seemed shocked by the wonder of it]—a library in Jalapa—the very first ever!

CORINTO, CHINANDEGA

Pedro Madriz, forty-eight, is a Corinto fisherman. Madriz is a short, slight man. His flower design shirt, tan flared trousers, and black simulated patent-leather shoes were flashy when new. Now, like Madriz, they are shabby and weatherworn.

Pedro Madriz

There have been many changes in my life since the Triumph. In the old days we fishermen could take the best of the catch for ourselves. The best fish we took home with us. Now you can't take a shrimp, not a bony little raton. Nothing. Is that right? Is that fair?

Before the Triumph I worked steady. I was always at sea. Now I haven't had one day's work in three months.

I worked on the same boat for the same company for thirteen years. I worked for the Alinsa Fishing Company. They had many, many boats. The Alinsa belonged to Bernabe Somoza, the nephew of Anastasio. He's probably in Miami now. No worries in his life.

In March I had my last day's work. Since then, nothing. Listen, I have six kids and my *compañera*. She's sick. What am I going to do? I had a little money saved, but now I'm down to my last 1,000 cordobas. After that's gone, who knows? I look everywhere for work, and I can't find a thing.

The problem is that we have no boats now. It's true that six of them have been damaged by the mines, but there's more to it than that. I think that the government . . . they don't know what they're doing.

I think that the main problem is poor administration. We have a couple of boats like that one, *The Pancisan*. It has a new engine in it, but they can't get it to work. Why? I don't know why. Who knows? Did you know that each boat that isn't working, each boat that's tied up at the wharf costs 2,000 cordobas a day? That's a lot of money.

We have a number of boats that are in good condition. But they've been taken over by the military for patrol work. How can you make a living on a boat, how can you be a fisherman, when the government takes the boats for patrol work? That doesn't do anybody any good.

I know one boat, though, that's being repaired. It'll be going to sea soon. Maybe they'll have a place for me. I'm going to find out.

I'm a net man myself. That's my rating. Our trips—we used to be fifteen to eighteen days at sea. Believe me when I tell you that I've caught my share of red snapper, curbina, robalo in my day. These waters here, they're full of first-class fish—if you can get to them.

Will things get better in Nicaragua? Sure, things will get better. When they get the boats working, when I get a job, when I make some money, things will be much better.

CIUDAD CHINANDEGA, CHINANDEGA

Maria Inez Gonzalez, thirty-one, is the dietician at the Francisco Dominguez Child Development Center in Chinandega City. She is of medium height, dark, on the stocky side. Gonzalez's eyes and her manner exude a keen intelligence and intensity. She wears a white smock and a cap.

We have eighty-four children here at the center. We have infants forty-five days old up to boys and girls six years old. Any working mother can bring her child here, especially if she has no man in her house or if she has no one to look after her child while she is at work.

The CDIs are different from anything we had in Nicaragua before the Triumph. In those days, poor mothers were forced to dump their children anywhere so that they could earn their living. Sometimes mothers carried their children to work with them in the most unpleasant, unhealthy environment. Many children were abandoned by desperate mothers. The system was full of brutality for mothers and children.

But that's history now. At Francisco Dominguez we provide a full program from eight o'clock in the morning until five in the afternoon. We give the children good meals. The clothing that they wear at the center, we provide. And most importantly, we give our children a total education, a cultural experience, in the most important years of their lives.

We have a large staff—sixteen workers for eighty-four children. That's something, isn't it? We have three preschool educators; three attend the babies; two women work in the nursery with the infants. We have a full-time dietician, a nurse, cooks, cleaning people, an economist, a watchman, and our coordinator. A total of sixteen.

This program is not charity—it isn't free. Everyone must pay according to her income. If a mother earns only 500 cordobas a month she pays 35. The minimum is 19 cordobas a month. We believe that it's important that everyone pays something. It increases their sense of responsibility.

Of course, the fees don't cover the costs at this or at any CDI. It is the responsibility of the government. The government provides the money necessary for the CDI program throughout Nicaragua.

I don't know how many CDIs there are in Nicaragua, but there are many of them throughout the country and their numbers are growing. I recently attended a seminar for CDI dieticians in Managua. There were people there from twenty-nine CDIs, from every department in Nicaragua. So you see, CDIs are a factor here.

In addition, we have a parallel program—the CDRs. That's Centro Desarrollo Rural. The CDRs are for the countryside, for the rural areas. I believe that the CDRs are not as numerous or advanced as we are. But, like everything else, it's just a matter of time—.

A burst of children's song momentarily overpowered our discussion. Nodding in the direction of the adjoining classroom, Gonzalez murmered, as though to herself,

And the gringos think they can come here and destroy all of this in a minute . . .

She looked into my eyes as though to gauge my response. I was noncommital. She finished her aside.

If we all die, at least we'll go to heaven.
You see, conditions in Nicaragua have changed—for everyone. For

the rich, for the poor, for city people and campesinos, for men and women, even for little babies.

My father was a campesino. My mother never so much as walked out of the house without asking his permission. You can see all of the education and opportunity that I, the daughter of such a family, have had. Before the Triumph women like me had almost no opportunity to study, to prepare ourselves for a professional career.

Now there is no limit for us. After formal education is completed, there are seminars, short courses. Wages, too, are uniform for men and women. Where else can that be said in Central America?

We have organizations exclusively for the betterment of women. AMNLAE, for instance. We are organized in every barrio in Chinandega. If women find that they have suffered discrimination because of their sex, we get involved. We fight for justice for women.

[I recalled the case of Lulu Gonzalez, in Ocotal—deserted by her husband, abused and beaten by him.] What do you do in a situation where a woman is beaten by her husband?

We don't like to get invoved in personal, famiiy matters.

What if she asked for your help?

In that case I would advise the woman to tell her husband that we are living a revolutionary process. Everyone has the right to have respect. That woman must go to the authorities—to the police. The revolutionary process will put him in his place. *[She gestured toward the adjoining room.]*

How can these children grow up to build a new, fair, socialist society if they live in an environment of bestiality?

INGENIO SAN ANTONIO, CHINANDEGA

Miguel Colindres, fifty, is a forklift operator at the huge Nicaragua State Sugar refinery, which is privately owned. He is of medium height, with gray-flecked hair and a pot belly, unusual for a Nicaraguan working man. Like workers everywhere, Colindres was pleased at the opportunity to "dog it" for a few minutes. We chatted on the loading dock, where he was working at the time. A number of others gathered around us, and from time to time Colindres looked to them for corroboration of various facts that he wished to present.

I started work at Nicaragua State Sugar on February 5, 1949, and I've been here ever since. There have been many changes since I

Girl with a chicken, the Esteli-Somoto bus

started at this place. Most of the changes, though, have taken place during the past five years, since we had the Triumph of the Revolution.

Take wages, for instance. Our salaries have increased very much. The problem, though, is that things are so expensive now that you can hardly tell the difference.

Most of the improvements have been in things other than wages— in benefits. Our union has been good in that respect. We belong to the Sindicato Ronaldo Altimarando. We're affiliated to the CST. All 7,500 people here belong to the Sindicato. They must belong. It's a condition of employment.

One important thing we have here is a commissary. You get food for your family at the commissary. It's the best quality food, and you pay about 50 percent less than you would on the outside. For a family of eight, every week you can get twelve pounds of rice, eight pounds of beans, six bars of soap, one gallon of oil, two pounds of salt. Meat and other things we buy on the outside, like everyone else. Everything we buy is subsidized by the company. For instance, a pound of rice in the market costs 3 cordobas, 80 centavos. We get it for 1 and 20. See, that's a subsidy. And it's all top quality stuff.

Another benefit here is for the old workers. Here we retire at sixty years. Before, when you retired they gave you a few cordobas and waved good-bye. Now the company gives you a home, a place to live out your life—rent-free. You get your pension and you also have the right to continue to buy your food at the commissary, subsidized. That's something, eh?

In case we get sick, they send us to the hospital. We have a hospital nearby, in Chinandega. If it's a serious illness they'll send you to Leon, or even to a hospital in Managua. It doesn't cost us a cordoba. Nothing. That's because it's subsidized.

Another thing, and this is good for the young people. Whoever wants to can study to improve himself. You get every opportunity to study so that you can qualify for a better job. Many of the young people do this.

Not me, though. I'm too old. In my free time I like to take a little drink sometimes. Also, I like to go to the movies. I like American pictures the best, especially westerns and war pictures. But I wouldn't walk from here to there to see a Ronald Reagan movie. Not if they paid me money.

You're an American. You tell that man to stop this war. Stop killing our people. Leave us in peace.

This part of Chinandega during the revolution was known as "The Red Zone." We had many struggles here. The biggest was on July 2, 1979, when our area was liberated from the Guardias. You tell Mr. Ronald Reagan that we picked up the gun then, and we'll do it again if we have to. But really, we don't want to fight anyone. Me, all I want to do is maybe sometimes take a little drink, go to the movies. You tell Mr. Reagan.

GRANADA

A brief exchange with a young woman, a Granada bank teller:

Are you a Sandinista?
Me? Never. Down with the Sandinistas!

Why?
Because they're Marxists, Communists.

What's a Communist?
Communists? They're Sandinistas. Maybe that's what you are, too!

LAS MANOS, NUEVA SEGOVIA

Manuel is forty-two years old. He is tall, broad, and has a quick and engaging smile.

I am Honduran—that is, I *was* Honduran. But now I live here in Nicaragua. See, here's my permanent residency card. So now I'm Nicaraguan.

I was a student in Honduras, in Tegucigalpa. I studied agriculture. But more than that, I was in the movement against the fascists in my country. I had to leave Honduras.

Now I'm a Nicaraguan. My wife is Nicaraguan, and my two children. I own a few manzanas of coffee here on the Honduran border. So you see, I use what I learned in a fascist country for socialism—against fascism.

I love this country, I'll never leave it. But if I wanted to go to Honduras, even for a visit to my mother, I couldn't. My brother-in-law, my sister's husband, he's a spy, an informer. That snake would turn me in for the price of a new sombrero.

Did you ever hear of Che Guevera? He was my hero. *La lucha continua . . .*

JALAPA, NUEVA SEGOVIA

Beyond the high forested mountains is Honduras, the sanctuary from which bands of counterrevolutionaries conduct frequent forays into this region. The timber industry in the hills is a thriving business, and the coffee groves on the cool hillsides are a principal source of foreign currency.

The lowlands are long, broad, and rich. The crops here are tobacco, sorghum, rice, and cotton. Before the Triumph these farms had been estates, owned by Somoza and those around him. Now some are state farms, others thriving cooperatives. Jalapa is indeed a prize, and there is daily, unremitting warfare between those who now own these riches and those who covet them.

On the main road, at the outskirts of town, is a 10-acre tractor park surrounded by a high wire fence. In the early morning scores of tractors, combines, harvesters—every manner of farm machine—roar through the gate and to area farms. In the early evening, their day's labor done, the drivers return their machines to the field, where they are placed under guard for the night.

During the daylight hours, teams of grease-monkeys, mechanics— youths, for the most part—repair and maintain idle equipment. The tractors' names are familiar: International Harvester, Ford, Massey- Ferguson, John Deere. Not so familiar are the newer acquisitions. Small, squat, fire-engine red Bela Ruses—Russian machines.

Natividad Ortiz is a tall, lean, curly-headed man of fifty- two. He is a "kidder," unique among Nicaraguan country people. They tend to be on the serious side.

Ortiz wears boots, blue jeans, a white sport shirt and "McGre- gor" baseball cap. He is a cho- fer, a driver, and he's happy to show off the tractor park. Ortiz climbs to the cab of a monster of a red machine and poses, smil- ing, for a picture.

Natavidad Ortiz

This little girl, it's the newest, the best, the biggest we have. A harvester—for rice. Very strong, very fast. Six manzanas an hour.

He climbs down to confront the North American and winks broadly.

Russian—the best.

All these machines—they're used by the cooperatives and state farms around here. They pay to use them—by the day. Everyone has to pay, even the government farms.

I'm a *chofer*. I'm the best, the most experienced. Before the Triumph I did the same kind of work. But then I worked for the big guys—the ones who owned these farms around here. After our Triumph they ran. They left Nicaragua. But the land—they left *it* behind. [*He laughs.*]

You've got a good job.

It beats working with the machete. [*We both laugh.*]

OCOTAL, NUEVA SEGOVIA

On a bluff overlooking the Luis Alfonso Velasquez Cooperative Farm is Maderero Yodeco, one of Nicaragua's most important sawmills. More than 350 people are employed at Yodeco, which processes some 14,000 feet of lumber daily.

The mill is a complex of shops and sheds spread out over a twenty-acre site. At the back of the property, overlooking the valley, is the saw and conveyor shed. There is a machine shop at Maderero Yodeco, a vulcanization shop, a lathe area that manufactures broom handles out of scrap lumber, an administration building, storage areas, and other, smaller, units. Most of the mill's production is used for housing construction and industry.

During their lunch break I spoke with four of the workers: Lionel Rivera, foreman, forty-three; Hiram Blandong, eighteen; Evenora Torres, nineteen; and Joseph Franklin, eighteen.

RIVERA: I'm the foreman on this shift. I've been working at the mill since I came to Ocotal. That was back in 1968. I'm from the Atlantic Coast, from Puerto Cabezas. There was no work there, no way to make a living. So I came to Ocotal, I got this job, I got married. I've been here ever since, for sixteen years.

Could you describe what it was like here before 1979, before the Triumph?

RIVERA: This mill used to be owned by North Americans, by the Braggman Lumber Company. They had Cubans, that is, ex-Cubans— what we call *gusanos*—running it for them. In those days the name of the mill was Maderero Magon. Just before the Triumph of the Revolution they took everything they could, all of the machinery. They shipped it to Guatemala and Brazil. What they couldn't move they burned. This place was a mess. All of the sheds, all of the buildings, burned to the ground.

Now it's owned by the government?
RIVERA: That's right. We own it. We started with nothing. A lot of work went into this mill. They say there's not a better one in Nicaragua. We built this place from the ground up.
TORRES: I helped to build Yodeco. Right after the Triumph. I was fourteen years old. I've been here since the first day.

What was it like to work here before?
RIVERA: Years ago old man Somoza said he wanted Nicaraguans to be oxen. The Cubans took him at his word. It was never steady work here. You'd work a week sometimes. Then they'd tell you to take the next week off. Or else you'd come in in the morning and they'd tell you "Go home, no work today." When you didn't work you didn't get paid. That happened very, very often. The pay—it was nothing.

And now?
RIVERA: Now at least we have security. We have our union—the CST. You have a job here as long as you want it. And the pay—I make four times what I did working for the Cubans. Of course, everything costs more now, so the money isn't *that* much better.

(To the young men) *Do you plan to continue to work here? [Torres and Blandong nod in the affirmative.]*
FRANKLIN: Next year I think I'm going to be gone. I think I'm going to go to Managua, to the university.
TORRES: Where are you going?
FRANKLIN: To the National University in Managua. Every night you *chavalos* are in the pool hall and I'm studying at the Institute. Why do you think I do that? Because I want to go to the university.
BLANDONG: I wouldn't mind going to the university. But I don't think so. There's going to be a war.

And if there is a war?
BLANDONG: If the Yankees come, or if they send someone else to invade us, I'll go in a minute. I'm in the militia.
TORRES: Who isn't in the militia?
RIVERA: We here, we're all in the militia. We train. We do *vigilancia*.

Young beauty, Corn Island, Zelaya

Is there a Juventud Sandinista in Ocotal?
TORRES: Certainly. We're all in the Juventud, too. All of the young people are.

Why are you in the Juventud?
TORRES: We all do sports. And the Juventud organizes everything. We have our Juventud baseball, basketball, volleyball . . .
BLANDONG: In the Junventud you're with your friends, your *compañeros*.
FRANKLIN: Also, we do good things.

What kind of good things?
FRANKLIN: We clean up the park. We fix the roads—all together—and then we have a fiesta. Sometimes we work with the little ones, with the Sandinista Children's Association. We do everything, all of our social activities, with the Juventud.
TORRES: You must understand. We're organized people. It's not every person for himself. Not in Nicaragua. Not anymore.

(To Rivera) *And what about the older people? People your age and older?*
RIVERA: You listen to these kids. They're smart—smarter than we were. Look, I earn four times as much money as I did when I worked for the Cubans. Things are tight but nobody troubles us. I myself, I'm not a Sandinista. But I understand certain things. My kids. I have a fourteen-year old in the fifth grade and a one-year-old baby. It's all for them. These kids here, they'll benefit.

No problems?
RIVERA: Things are tight. But that's not the government's fault. The imperialists are blockading us, and they force us to spend our foreign exchange on guns instead of parts and other things that we need. So we have to make do with what we have. We improvise. When we have to we do without.

The discussion above took place on May 30, 1984. Two days later, on June 1, Ocotal was raided by some 500 Honduras-based contras. Maderero Yodeco, a granary, a coffee-processing plant, and the radio station, were the prime targets.

I visited the sawmill two days later, on June 3. Maderero Yodeco was totally destroyed. The machinery was burned, twisted beyond repair. All of the sheds, the buildings, were burned—they still smoldered.

Seven weeks later, on July 22, I returned to Maderero Yodeco. The sawmill, working on a reduced schedule, had been partially rebuilt, operating with machinery salvaged from mills elsewhere in Nicaragua. Some of the sheds had been rebuilt, and there was regular, although limited, production.

I sought out Lionel Rivera. He informed me that three days after the attack, when the area had cooled sufficiently, the work force had been called back to begin cleanup. Within a week reconstruction of the sheds had begun. Four weeks later replacement machinery had arrived and assembly started. He wryly reminded me that was the second time the mill had been destroyed by agents of my countrymen.

Hiram Blandong, too, was back at work at Maderero Yodeco. Evenora Torres and Joseph Franklin had been called up by the militia. At the time of our meeting they were stationed near the Honduran border. From others I learned that Rivera had been marked by the Frente Democratica Nicaraguense (FDN), the political arm of the contras, for assassination. For his role in the reconstruction and restored production at the mill he has been targeted to be murdered as an enemy of "Free Nicaragua."

SOMOTO, MADRIZ

Santos Rivera Sanchez is sixty-four years old. He is tall, spare, with a neatly trimmed gray mustache. He was resting, watching children at play in the park in Somoto.

I used to have a farm near here. I was born here, and I raised my family here—two sons and four daughters. Now my children are scattered. They're in Esteli, Managua, all over.

I had forty manzanas, all planted in tobacco. I got my first fifteen manzanas from my father when I was a young man. The rest I bought a little at a time, over the years. Some of this land was new land. I cleared it and I planted tobacco. I built two tobacco barns.

I made a fair living from tobacco. Some years it was better, other times it was not so good. We all worked very hard—my wife, me, my children. So we did pretty well.

Near my farm were many big ones, most of them in tobacco. One time my neighbor said to me, "Santos, sell me your land. I'll give you a good price."

But I said, "Why should I sell? I'm happy here. I make a good living. I feed my family. No, I'll keep my land."

Street kid, Ocotal, Nuevo Segovia

This neighbor, he was a rich man, very strong. He was in with the Somoza gang.

When it came time to plant my next crop, I went to the bank for a loan. We farmers live on credit. We have land, tobacco, many things, but we never have the money to plant a crop. So we go to the bank.

But this time the bank said no. I asked why not? They had lent me money every year. I always paid my debt.

But they wouldn't tell me why they wouldn't lend me money this time. All they said was "No, no, no."

Then I understood. This was a Somoza bank. This neighbor was in with Somoza. Okay. So I went to another bank. But it was the same thing. No discussion. Just "No, no, no."

I borrowed money from my family. I borrowed from friends. I sold some things. I raised the money and I planted my tobacco. Maybe you think the story is finished, but it isn't.

Bus, Santo Tomas, Chontales

I planted my tobacco and it was a good crop. I filled two barns with tobacco. Then one night one of my barns burned. Mysteriously. Was it an accident? But I knew better. My neighbor had burned my barn.

What could I do? Where could I turn? Could I go to the police? Could I get a lawyer? I couldn't. They would all laugh at me. You see, the Somoza people were tight together. If they wanted your eye, they took it. If they wanted your land, they took it. You could do nothing.

Now I'm an old man. I'm retired. I live with my daughter and her husband and their three children. He works on the land and she has a stall in the market. I help her in the market. Sometimes I watch my grandchildren.

I visit my other children. Last year I went to see my daughter in Managua. I have a good life, better than before.

There are many shortages. Certain kinds of food are hard to get. Other things, too. But it's better than before. Now no one steals anything. This government is based upon fairness to the people.

My old land is now owned by the government, or maybe it's a cooperative farm. I'm not sure which. My old neighbor, he's in Miami or someplace like that. He couldn't take my land with him, though, could he?

4
THE ATLANTIC COAST

Looking Out on the Caribbean: Mines, Miskitos and Reggae

Don't let the Sandinistas vaccinate you.
Don't allow them to vaccinate your children.
The Sandinistas use two types of serum: one to
sterilize you, the other turns you into a
Communist.

If you have a scrap of food and must choose
between giving it to a dog or a Sandinista, give
it to the dog. A dog can be a faithful friend. A
Sandinista is always treacherous.

—Steadman Faggoth, ex-Somoza agent
and now a principal leader of the
counter-revolutionary FDN,
Miskito-language radio broadcasts from
Honduras

PUERTO CABEZAS

Without warning, as though to demonstrate its waspish perversity, the sky opened and a deluge fell on the baked dirt streets of Puerto Cabezas. On the Atlantic Coast, between May and August, this happens once, twice, five times daily.

Sometimes at midday it rains for one minute, barely blotting the sun's relentless glare. More often it persists for ten to fifteen minutes, and then steam rises from the city's few paved streets.

Only during the late afternoon and in the evening does the rain provide a measure of relief in this soggy, steamy land. Then, combined with the cool breeze blowing in from the ocean, this shabby, frontier-like town of 15,000 is relatively comfortable.

In the park in the town's center, on this late afternoon, raindrops slapped the hot concrete walk without warning. Thirty or more people rushed to the protection of the roofed gazebo. They were Mestizos,

Miskitos, Blacks, Creoles—a good-natured crowd, young for the most part. They seemed grateful for this easily acquired protection from the rain and for the relief that would follow. Their sense of community was stirred by the common discomfort and its simple remedy.

Lightning flashed, followed by thunder, and then a raucous, voice shouted, "Sandinista rain. Anything to discomfort the people." The voice was rough but had an edge of good humor. The speaker was a heavily bearded Black man of perhaps forty. Dishevelled and ragged, he was a familiar sight in the park—the village iconoclast.

A young voice shot back: "Sandinista? What do you know? You're never sober enough to know the difference between Sandinista and Santa Maria."

Someone in the crowd tittered. The second speaker was hidden from my view.

"Look who's talking," the first man returned. "A boy your age. You should respect your elders."

"Rave on, Mr. Reagan," the lad retorted. Now I saw him, a boy of perhaps sixteen. A Miskito, he wore a broad-brimmed olive camouflage hat and other military odds and ends. Probably, I assumed, in the militia.

"When you start to shave you can have opinions. Then you can debate with a man of my experience."

"Opinions? Like you? Never!"

They had moved closer, nose to nose. Many in the crowd laughed.

"Idiot."

"Double idiot."

"Stupid."

"Drunken fool."

"Cretin."

The crowd roared with laughter.

"Burro."

The supreme insult: "You can take the Indian out of the bush, but you can't take the bush out of the Indian."

"Rave on drunken fool. Mouthpiece for Ronald Reagan."

The rain stopped as suddenly as it had begun. The crowd, the antagonists among them, dispersed as though by signal, down the steps of the gazebo, to their friends, to their evening's pleasure.

———— ♦ ————

Nubia Mora, twenty-four, is a secretary with long dark black hair. She is a pleasant woman with an easy smile.

My father gave my mother twelve children—five girls and seven boys—and then he died. I was the youngest in the family. I don't remember him.

I tell you the truth, I don't know how we managed to stay alive. My mother made fruit drinks in the house, and she sold them on the street. My brothers sold newspapers, they shined shoes, they worked here and there. Sometimes one of the boys "found" a piece of meat or a fish. Then there was a fiesta in our house. For the girls there was no possible work. You couldn't even clean other people's houses or do their washing. Grown women did that work. We girls helped my mother with her fruit drinks. We tried to make ourselves useful to her.

We kept chickens, so sometimes there was an egg or two, but we chidren didn't know what milk looked like. We were raised on rice and beans, rarely anything else. It was very difficult, but somehow my mother managed to keep us together, to keep us alive, to feed us, to send us to school.

I was nineteen at the time of the Triumph. During the war I had been attracted to the FSLN, to the things that they said about fighting for the poor. We learned about them from Radio Sandino. Also, sometimes someone from the Frente came to Puerto Cabezas, to our barrio. It was very dangerous, but he would come into someone's home at night. Then, ten or twelve people, or as many as could squeeze into the room, listened to him. He explained about the war, about the revolution, about the need for poor people to stay together. It sounded very good.

There was never any fighting in Puerto Cabezas. The war was in the west, on the Pacific side, so there was very little that we could do here.

After the Triumph the FSLN came to Puerto Cabezas, and there were many changes. Before, many women became pregnant. Often, the man just walked away. Now the government forces him to pay for the children. Before, for women, there was nothing. Now every girl goes to school. If she shows promise and the desire, she is encouraged to continue her education. There is no limit to what a woman can achieve now.

Take prostitution. Before, prostitution was a scourge in Puerto Cabezas. Sailors from all over the world came here, and they and the

Miskito women of Kukra Hill, Zelaya

prostitutes took over the streets. Every street had prostitutes. Every fourth, fifth house was the home of a prostitute. What could a girl do? How could she feed herself? There was no decent work for women. There was nothing.

Now there is very little prostitution, almost none. Why should a girl be a prostitute now? There is education and work for everyone.

Myself, I'm in the *vigilancia*. I go on patrol in my barrio one night a week. Sometimes from six to nine o'clock, sometimes from nine to midnight. Or else I go from midnight to three o'clock or from three to six in the morning.

There are eight or twelve of us together, and I enjoy *vigilancia*. We walk the streets and see that there is no antisocial behavior. Before, it was terrible here. You couldn't walk in the street at night without getting robbed, even murdered. The criminals used to break into homes all the time and rob people at gunpoint.

Now you can go anywhere, anytime, in Puerto Cabezas. You can go with confidence. People sleep good here now.

I'm not in the FSLN. I'd like to be more active, but with three children it is difficult. The children need attention. Also, my husband is in the patriotic military service. He serves right here in Puerto Cabezas. For now, I think that's enough for our family.

———— ♦ ————

Clifford Blanford is a tall, broad, Black man. He is thirty-eight years old. Blanford is a handsome fellow. He is easygoing, relaxed, and obviously enjoys talking with a foreign writer.

I had an uncle who worked in Rosita, in the mine. In those days they were mining copper in Rosita. The mine was owned by a Canadian company—I forget the name.

One day my aunt, his wife, came to visit us. We were living in Bluefields—that's where I was born. My aunt asked me, "Clifford, how would you like to work in the mine with your uncle?"

I was seventeen years old then, and I wasn't doing much of anything. So I said, "Sure, why not?"

A couple of weeks later came a letter from my aunt. Said, "Come on up to Rosita. Plenty work, good pay."

So I went on up to Rosita. It was a good job in the mine. Good pay. In those days the price of copper was high. You see, Rosita has copper *and* gold. In the later years, when the price of copper went way down, they switched over to gold mining.

I worked in Rosita for about a year. But then I got homesick for Bluefields, so I went home.

I stayed in Bluefields for about three or four months. Now, my dad—when I was growing up, he worked on a ship; he worked for the INSCO Shipping Company for many years. My dad was home at that time. And he said to me, "Clifford, I'm tired of going to sea. Let's both go on up to Rosita and see if we can get some work."

So we went back to Rosita. He got a job driving a tractor. I got work in the kitchen, as a waiter. After a while I got a job as second cook, then first cook. I'll tell you something. I was a *bad* cook [laughs]. No, I never killed anyone, but I think some of them got pretty sick.

I stayed working at the mine for seventeen years. I married a girl from Rosita. Had four kids.

After the Triumph they closed the kitchen down, and I was out of a job. Then, soon after that, the price of gold went way down, and because they had such small reserves they closed the whole operation down. I think now it's started up again. Not full capacity, but working.

Anyway, when I lost my job at the mine I got a job in the sawmill in Rosita—CORFOP. It's owned by the government. That job was good. I'm pretty lucky—I always got good jobs. I worked there for about two years until they moved the sawmill to Limbaika.

I didn't want to go to Limbaika because I didn't want to leave my family. I didn't want to leave Rosita. You see, I'd built a pretty good life for myself in Rosita. I was the head of the CDS in my barrio—28th of May. We had a good CDS—we worked together. We kept the streets clean. We fixed the water system. We even made a lot of improvements in the park.

Also, I was going to school. I was learning the Miskito language. Lots of Miskitos in Rosita, and I've always worked with them. I like those people a lot, and I always wanted to talk better, to know them better. So I was going to school nights to learn the language better.

Anyway, I stayed on in Rosita when the sawmill moved to Limbaika. The new sawmill in Limbaika was attacked by contras soon after it got started. It burned to the ground. So you see, I would have been out of a job anyway.

Now I needed a job and I couldn't find one in Rosita. So I came up here to Puerto Cabezas to find one. I work at COMAPECO. We make prefabricated houses, out of wood. They're nice houses. Some with two, some with three rooms—and a bathroom.

But now I'm here, and they—my family—they're in Rosita. I don't know exactly what I'm going to do. Probably I'll move them here, but I'm not sure. I miss them, but I don't like Puerto Cabezas. I like Rosita. I like living in the bush. Also, the price of everything here is too high. Take plantains. In Rosita you might pay 2 or 3 cordobas for a plantain. Here, the same plantain will cost you 8 cordobas.

The reason everything costs less in Rosita is that there are a lot of good farms all around. They grow plenty of everything. Even got good cattle around Rosita. Nothing much growing around Puerto Cabezas. Everything has to come in by boat from Bluefields. That costs money.

Also, I don't want to move my family from Rosita because of the war. Everything is so unsettled. The war—I'm scared to death about it. I don't see any signs of peace, so I'm very worried.

My oldest son, he's fifteen, and he lives in Bluefields with his aunt. He goes to school there, and his aunt has just taken him over. She won't let go of him. I think I lost that boy [laughs]. Anyway, I worry about my boy, about the military. Of course, if he has to go . . .

I support this government. I think it has some good programs. In Rosita, for instance, the hospital is bigger than before. We have more

FROM:

LIBRARY RATE

TO:

INTERLIBRARY LOAN SERVICE
SEELEY G. MUDD LEARNING CENTER
OBERLIN COLLEGE
OBERLIN, OHIO 44074

RETURN POSTAGE GUARANTEED—ADDRESS CORRECTION REQUESTED

MAY BE OPENED FOR POSTAL INSPECTION IF NECESSARY

_____ PARCEL POST   _____ EXPRESS COLLECT
_____ PREINSURED   _____ EXPRESS PREPAID
$ _____ VALUE

doctors, more teachers. Young people go to the university now. My daughter, I think she wants to go to the university.

You take my job. We make twelve prefabricated houses a day. That's good. Nicaragua needs houses for people. They're expanding so that next year we'll be able to produce twice as much, maybe twenty-four, twenty-five houses a day. That's a good program. That's very good for Nicaragua. Every place you look you see programs like that.

They're fixing the streets, putting in good water. They're trying hard. You can't fault them for that. Of course, they make mistakes, too. If you're human, you make mistakes. Isn't that so?

Lydia, my wife, and me talk about this a lot. We both have the same ideas about things. We both support the government. Take crime. Now there are very few thieves. Before the revolution—oh, boy.

Then there was discrimination here. Since the Triumph we seem to mix better. We have more of a Christian brotherhood now. I like that. If we believe in God, we try to help our brother. In the CDS in Rosita that's what we did—we worked together as Christians. Anyway, that's the way I always looked at it.

———— ♦ ————

Justos Smith Ingle, forty-three, is a Miskito Indian. He is a tall, lean, brooding man, dark and with a full black mustache.

The first time I saw the helicopter—I didn't know it then, but I know it now—that was the end of my town, of Cabo Gracias.

I was born in Cabo Gracias—Cape Grace. That's near the Wanka River. It's way up in the north, across from Honduras. Cabo Gracias is also near the ocean.

Cabo Gracias was a pretty big place. At one time we had 900 homes. But then in 1971 we had a hurricane. It blew down many houses. Many people were killed—forty-five, I think. Then many people left Cabo Gracias after the hurricane. After that we had about 500 houses—500 families.

After I grew up, when I was a man, I rarely left Cabo Gracias. When I was a boy, though, I traveled a lot. I knew this city well. I came to Puerto Cabezas often. I dived for lobster around here. One time I lived in Puerto Cabezas for almost a year. I worked in a sawmill. I made some money, and then I went home. I always returned to Cabo Gracias.

Life was good in Cabo Gracias. It was my home. I had some land. Later I got married; I had four children. My mother and my grand-mother, they lived with me.

We had what we needed. We had cassava, rice, beans, bananas, coconut, breadfruit. There were plenty of fish in the river and in the streams. In the ocean we had shrimp and turtle—sometimes shark. Around Cabo Gracias there were lots of animals in the forest. We never lacked food or anything else that we needed. I had twenty-eight head of cattle. My brother, Tom Smith, he had forty-five cattle. Tom's in Costa Rica now.

We all knew that there had been a war in Nicaragua. We also knew that there was a new government. But that didn't mean anything to me—the new government. To me it was all the same.

In 1980, 1981, people came across to us from Honduras. They told us that the Sandinistas were going to kill us. They said that the Sandinistas were going to destroy all of the Miskito people. They said that the Sandinistas hated us and that they wanted our land, so they were going to wipe us out. They told us to go to Honduras. In Honduras, they said, we would be safe.

Many people did that. Our people were very frightened. They left in the middle of the night, and they walked. It was less than one-hour walk to the river. Then they'd go across by dug-out, to Honduras.

You see, there have always been many Miskito people in Honduras, and I know that they have always been safe there. They never were troubled by anyone. I, myself, have cousins, uncles who live in Honduras. They live well. They were never troubled by anyone.

I would have gone to Honduras, too. But I couldn't. I had my grandmother. She was ninety-six years old and she was blind. She was also very fat. How could I take this old woman through the forest? How could I take her across the river in a dug-out?

After the helicopter came from Honduras, the government soldiers came to Cabo Gracias. They told us we had to leave right now, right away. We couldn't take as much as a spoon with us from Cabo Gracias—only the clothes we wore. From Cabo Gracias we had to walk to Bismona. That was a full day's walk. It was very hard. My grandmother and some of the other older ones, the sick people, they put in jeeps.

They say that after we left Cabo Gracias the government soldiers burned our houses and shot our cattle and ate them. I don't know. I haven't been back there.

In Bismona they put us on trucks to Waspam. That was a one-and-one-half-hour ride. From Waspam they took us to Trujlaya. That was a four-and-one-half-hour trip.

Trujlaya was a *campamiento*—a camp. From the first we didn't like it. We hated that place. Everyone was frightened, crying. Many people were sick. The government soldiers didn't kill us or beat us or hurt us. But it was a terrible place. Trujlaya was so hot—it was so strange. Many people were sick, people were dying. My grandmother died in Trujlaya.

Later they destroyed Trujlaya. They took the houses down and moved them to Columbo, which I'm told is a better place. But this was later.

At Trujlaya I begged them to let us go. If we couldn't go home to Cabo Gracias, then we would come here to Puerto Cabezas. I knew Puerto Cabezas. I could work here as I had done before. I could take care of my family here.

We were in Trujlaya for four months and fifteen days. Then they said, "You can go. But not to the north—not to Cabo Gracias." So we came here to Puerto Cabezas. We have been here since that time.

I built a house for my family in Barrio Moyé. It wasn't too bad. Then I went to work. I dived for lobster, as I did when I was a boy. But then the lobster boat stopped coming. I don't know why.

I had a little money from the lobsters and I went to Corn Island. I bought some coconuts and I sold them here in the market. Sometimes I buy turtles and fish from the dory people and I sell them in the market.

But it is very hard in Puerto Cabezas. Money is everything. If you haven't got money, you're nothing. There's no cassava here. There's no beans or rice in the fields. You need money for everything.

We must go back—return to our homes in Cabo Gracias. If it's true that my house is burned, all right. I'll build another. I can start up a herd of cattle again. The land is still there, and it's a good place. That's the most important thing.

They tell me that the Miskito people have a good life in Honduras. But I know that Miskito people are returning from Honduras to Nicaragua. I don't know who to believe, what to believe.

A man, today, he gave me some black coral to sell. Tomorrow I'm going to the mines. I'm going to Rosita and Bonanza to sell the coral. Maybe I can make a few cordobas.

———— ♦ ————

Florence Grant is eighty-four years old. A stately Creole, she walks with painful difficulty, leaning on a cane. Ms. Grant has recently been discharged from the hospital after being treated for a broken hip. She sputters with anger.

They did this to me. *They* broke my hip.

They? Who is they?
You know. Those people in Managua. *Them.*

How did they break your hip?
I went to the store to buy some meat. And, as usual, there was nothing there. No meat. So I rushed out of the store. I practically ran down the road. Well, I was so angry with *them*—so disgusted—that I fell into a hole in the road. I fell. I broke my hip. So you see, *they* did this to me. *They* broke my hip.

———— ♦ ————

Leonore Perez Bency, nineteen, is a Miskito, a machine operator in a Puerto Cabezas factory that manufactures cheap rings, necklaces, and other trinkets. A proletarian one generation removed from the bush, Ms. Perez is a free-willed Miskito and disciplined Sandinista; Miskito tribalist and Nicaraguan nationalist; a factory clock-puncher and Indian wanderer with a longing for the bright lights of Managua and New York. Her language is a blend, too, a patois of Miskito, Spanish, and Caribbean English.

Leonore Perez Bency

Informed of Ms. Grant's antipathy to the Sandinista government, Ms. Perez responds. "Fuck she!"

———— ♦ ————

A Creole man in his early sixties, the proprietor of a small general store. He is nervous, hesitant.

Puerto Cabezas shopkeeper

I was born in Pearl Lagoon. When I was seventeen years old I came to Puerto Cabezas. I had a sister living here. My sister was married to a German who had a contract to cut and sell timber to an American company. I worked with him for about six months.

Then I decided to go to Prinzapolka. The Long Leaf Timber Company, also American, was very busy down in that area. So I went to work for them. It wasn't bad work, but after about four months I decided to work for myself. From that day to this I've never worked for another man. I think I was about nineteen years old then.

I started to bake cakes and pies. I enjoyed that. It became my profession. I got a stand in the street, and I sold cakes and pies to the timber workers. You see, in addition to Long Leaf, there were other, smaller companies working around Prinzapolka. We had Creoles, Miskitos, Blacks, Spaniards—everyone. We all got along good.

Soon I started to make rice and beans, bread, and different kinds of meat and fish, too. It was a good business. I made a good living. That's because people have always liked my cooking. Then I got married. I started to have children, a family.

Further up the Prinzapolka River there is a town named Alamikamba. In those days there was a big company there—the La Luz Company. It was a Nicaraguan company. La Luz did gold mining, cut timber, had a sawmill. It was involved with many things. Later, I think, it was taken over by Canadians, or maybe Americans. I'm not sure which.

In Alamikamba I started a big store. I sold everything—clothes, rum, shoes, tools—everything. But also I made and sold food. Because I did many things in my life, but I'm really, by profession, a baker.

I raised my children in Alamikamba. I had grandchildren, and I lived there all these years. Until two years ago.

It's very hard to describe. You see, I support this government. Around Alamikamba, Prinzapolka, Limbaika, and other places along the river there are some people who don't support the government. There are counterrevolutionaries. They are armed. They get guns—I think from Honduras. These people started to bother me.

First, they tried to force other people to stop buying from me. That didn't work for them. Most of the people continued to buy from me. Then I had some broken windows and other damage. You see, they were trying to get my sons to join them against the government. But my sons, my family, they all support the government.

Then one of my sons disappeared. Just like that. He disappeared.

Methodist minister, Bluefields, Zelaya

For two years we haven't heard from him. I can't say that they killed him. I don't know. We don't know what became of him.

Soon after my son disappeared I left everything. I took my entire family here. My wife, my children, my grandchildren. You see, I have a large family, and I was afraid that something would happen to them. We rent this store. It's hard, but we manage. Here, at least, we have peace.

My son is gone. I don't know if I'll ever see him again. I'm an old man, but I worry about my family.

———— ◆ ————

At a Puerto Cabezas kindergarten the work table was placed under a large shade tree. The children, Miskitos, were busily engaged with crayon and paper. The lesson consisted of coloring in the big, block letters "FLSN."

Responding to a comment about the political nature of the assignment, the teacher, a woman in her early twenties, said, "We must be vigilant. All Nicaraguans. Even children. Remember, we are under attack by the most powerful, most warlike, most aggressive nation in the world."

———— ◆ ————

Abner Figueroa Hernandez, thirty-two, is the Puerto Cabezas Regional CDS coordinator. He works as a schoolteacher. Figueroa is of medium height, thin. He is an intense, harrassed-looking young man.

I'm not from the Atlantic Coast region. I was born in Matagalpa. My father was a shopkeeper. He had a store where he sold men's clothing. Gloria Galiano, my wife, is also from the Pacific region. She's from Rio San Juan, in the south. Gloria's a schoolteacher, too. She works in the primary school. I teach a course in electricity at the Instituto Nacional Heroes y Martires de Puerto Cabezas.

We came here from Waspam in 1981. Waspam was maybe the most important Miskito community in Zelaya. But now, with the war, Waspam has been evacuated. It's a military post. The entire region along the Rio Coco is now a military zone. It's our major line of defense against the counterrevolutionaries based in Honduras.

In Waspam I made my living as a radio repairman. The main reason I was there though, was the CDS. I was the coordinator in Waspam, too, the same as here. But when Waspam was evacuated I was assigned to the Puerto Cabezas region.

Life here on the coast, the struggle, it's difficult. But it's rewarding. I wouldn't want to be anyplace else now. Here we see growth. The people's consciousness is growing—their political development. Now every barrio—almost every barrio—has a CDS organization. When I came here three years ago there was almost nothing. There was no organization to speak of. That's changing. That's exciting for us to see.

Now we have indigenous—Indian—leadership in Puerto Cabezas. That's what my work is all about. That's crucial. Before, the Miskitos thought of themselves only as Miskitos—nothing more. There was no national consciousness. Now many—more every day—see themselves as Miskitos *and* as Nicaraguans. That's the basis for our work here— to bring the Miskito people into the mainstream of Nicaraguan society. To bring them into the twentieth century. To be a part of the process. To help them to benefit from the Triumph of the Revolution.

Miskito family, Puerto Cabezas

Before the Triumph, in the bush, they were dying in childbirth, of appendicitis. They had no medical care to speak of. They had a life span of forty to fifty years. They were dominated by superstition, fear. That's no way to live. Not now. Not in the new Nicaragua.

Of course, I don't want to paint a picture of Paradise. We've made mistakes in dealing with the Miskitos, and we're paying for them now. Many Miskitos have gone over to the other side. That's a tragedy. It's a tragedy that they permit themselves to be used by the imperialists. But we have an ongoing amnesty for Miskitos who lay down their arms. They'll return. Life is the best teacher. Isn't that so?

I must admit that my life, my work, has its difficulties in Puerto Cabezas. It's frustrating. For example, there is the language. Remember, two-thirds of the population of Puerto Cabezas is Miskito, and many of them speak only Miskito. I can't speak with them. I'd like to learn the Miskito language, but who has the time? Every day, every evening, there are meetings, discussions, work in the barrios. Work, work, work, seven days a week. I don't have time to breathe. My children—I have three—sometimes I don't see them for days.

What kind of work do we do in the Miskito barrios? Everything, anything that affects the life of the people. That's what the CDS does.

To learn specifically about what the CDS does, you must come to a CDS meeting. See for yourself, firsthand, how it works. You come with me to Barrio Moyé, a totally Miskito barrio. Learn for yourself about how the CDS works among the Miskito people.

I'll tell you something. Nicaragua's survival depends upon a politically informed, militant people. And that includes the Miskito people.

Me personally? I'll stay here in Puerto Cabezas for as long as I'm needed here. If I'm needed elsewhere, I'll go there. It's difficult to move my family here, there. It's a struggle. But life is a struggle. Isn't that so?

—————— ♦ ——————

Barrio Moyé is the largest Miskito community in Puerto Cabezas. It is also perhaps the poorest. At its eastern edge Moyé runs for three miles or more alongside the ocean. Bordering the beach, to a thickness of about a mile, is a forested belt. It is from these woods that most of the people of Barrio Moyé make their living. They gather and cut timber, process it in the woods, and sell the charcoal in the market.

The people of Barrio Moyé had traditionally been fishermen. But with the war, the scarcity of fuel and engines, the dangers of deep-sea voyaging, the fear of mines, and much more, this occupation is now denied them. And so the men fish close in to shore solely to supplement their meager fare of beans, rice, and tortillas.

On the near side of the forest is a large ragged field, and it is here, scattered haphazardly, that the Miskito people have their rough, stilted houses. The houses on a knoll at the southern portion of the field are newer. These are the homes of almost one-half of the population of a thousand families. The newcomers are refugees from the now abandoned traditional Miskito communities of the Rio Coco.

The highest point of Barrio Moyé is the site of the Moravian church. From the church porch, by far the largest building in the community, one can see all of Barrio Moyé. To the east one can make out the gentle Caribbean, the rough scrub forest, and the crude Miskito houses. The

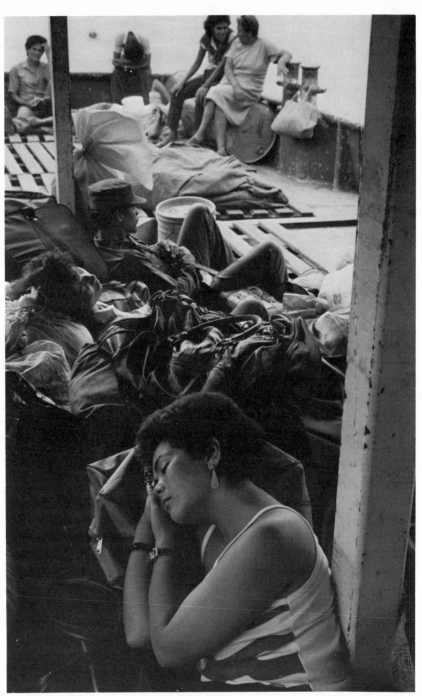

Passengers on the Bluefields-Rama boat

field is dotted by grazing horses and burros. Close into and under the houses are the dogs, chickens, pigs. Children, too, the smallest ones naked, are occupied around and under the houses.

On this late afternoon the hottest part of the day has passed. The weather has been gentled by the cool ocean breeze. In twos and threes, people—families, friends—walk slowly along the well-worn trail, up the hill to the church, mothers carrying infants. Children of all sizes mingle with their parents in the field alongside the prominent wooden building.

The Barrio Moyé Sandinista Defense Committee is scheduled to meet this evening. An important bit of business is to be resolved. The CDS assistant secretary, a young man, is to be replaced. Roger, married and the father of two children, has been absent for four months. A new assistant secretary is to be found to replace him.

Roger, it seems, had decided to take passage on a boat to Corn Island. He had planned to purchase a load of coconuts for resale in Puerto Cabezas. This venture, even given the difficulty of securing return passage—there is no regular schedule—should have taken one, two weeks at the most. But four months?

Three months ago a traveler reported seeing Roger happily working in Pearl Lagoon as a hand on a fishing boat. Then, six weeks later, he was reported seen in Kukra Hill, laboring in the sugar harvest. Roger, in the tradition of his people, has chosen to see a bit of the world hopefully to return eventually with a pocketful of cordobas for his family. There is no doubt that Roger will return. But in the meantime the Barrio Moyé Sandinista Defense Committee is short one leading cadre. A replacement must be found.

Soon, in the twilight, a hundred or more people are gathered in the field adjacent to the church. A half-dozen young mothers sit on the wooden steps, talking softly. Some nurse their babies. A number of older boys and girls, pre-teenagers, sit off on the side, in the field, chatting. Most, however, men and women of all ages, gather in a circle in the lee of the Moravian church.

In the circle's center stand two men—Abner Figueroa, the regional CDS coordinator, and Gaston Briones Vargas, a husky thirty-seven-year old Miskito. For some reason Briones is known to his neighbors as "Angry Bull." Gentle and soft-spoken, his demeanor belies the colorful nickname.

The meeting begins in both Spanish and the Miskito language, but as the evening wears on and the discussion grows intense, Spanish is all but abandoned.

A young Black man, Arthur Hudson, married to a Miskito, and chuckling thoughout most of the meeting, offers to interpret for me. Hudson is fluent, as are many in this region, in the three principal languages.

Figueroa—Briones translating into the soft, fluid Miskito language—lays out the problem. Roger is a good man, a good Nicaraguan. He has been an outstanding CDS leader—and will be again, no doubt. But now he is absent and must be replaced as assistant secretary. The assembled people are asked to nominate a replacement for Roger. Then a vote will be taken and a new CDS cadre elected.

The audience listens politely. All seem to understand perfectly. All seem to agree to the business at hand.

Hardly have Figueroa/Briones opened the meeting than a squat,

Miskito, Sumobila

animated, middle-aged woman steps forward, the mother of the errant Roger.

"I told my sons to have nothing to do with the CDS. They have to work to earn money for their families. That's the most important. That comes first. My son Roger worked hard for the CDS. What did he gain from it? Nothing. That's why I told him, 'Roger, take care of your family. That comes first.' "

Satisfied, smiling broadly, nodding her head, she returns to her place. Some of the people smile. Now a young man in his mid-twenties steps to the center of the circle.

"Someone told me that now we're going to need papers, a license, to sell charcoal in the market. Is that true? How much will the license cost?"

"That's not true," replies Briones softly. "We will not need a license to sell our charcoal."

A woman shouts angrily, "Who told you that?"

The young man responds in a low voice, "It was told to me in confidence."

"Yes, in confidence," she shouts back. "That's a lie. That's how the counterrevolutionaries try to make us angry with the government. They lie. Bring him here, the Somocista. Let him tell his lies openly, to the people."

Briones holds up his hand. "Compañeros. Let's get on with the business at hand."

An older man speaks up. "At the last meeting it was decided to establish a Barrio Moyé fishing cooperative. That's good. The problem is it costs 600 cordobas to join. That's crazy. Who here has 600 cordobas? Who has 500 cordobas? Who has 300 cordobas?"

Another and older man steps forward. "How can we have a fishing cooperative? There's no ice. You can't get ice in Puerto Cabezas."

But the first man is not to be put off. "—Who has 100 cordobas? Who has 50 cordobas to spare to become a member of the fishing cooperative?"

Now, in small groups, the people start talking among themselves. Each animatedly discusses the degree of his poverty. This evokes an air of general merriment.

Once again Briones pleads for order, for a return to the business of choosing a new assistant secretary.

A volatile, broadly built man speaks up. "When I was assistant secretary I wore out my shoes walking, walking. Now, if the CDS had bought me a new pair of shoes . . ."

Immediately, a woman carrying a baby in her arms responds. "If we want a new assistant secretary, I think it's only fair that we pay something to him. For his shoes. For other things."

The crowd murmurs assent.

Now Figueroa, Briones interpreting, speaks earnestly, passionately. He stresses the voluntary nature of CDS. He talks in terms of community spirit, patriotic duty, Nicaragua's—Somoza's—legacy of corruption and self-seeking, the development of New Socialist Man, and much more. The crowd seems genuinely touched. As Figueroa/Briones wind down, there is a scattering of applause.

The young woman with the baby is not to be put off. "I make a motion that every family in Barrio Moyé contribute 5 cordobas each month for the secretary and the assistant secretary. Everyone who agrees should raise his hands."

Almost every hand immediately rises.

Once again Figueroa/Briones plead with the audience. Such a motion could not be accepted, is out of order. The voluntary nature of the Sandinista Defense Committees is once again invoked.

Hardly satisfied, confused, the crowd nevertheless acquiesces.

Once again the mother of the errant Roger steps to the circle's center. "Believe me, if I could read and write, I would take the assistant secretary job in a minute. And the first thing I would do is I would go around this barrio and tell people to clean up around their houses. This place is filthy. What's the matter with you people? Why don't you clean up outside your houses?"

There is general laughter, but it is short-lived. For now another woman speaks up. "There's no milk in the barrio, no milk in Puerto Cabezas. Why didn't the boat from Bluefields come this week? I think we ought to do a petition. Let's tell those people in Managua. . . ."

There is a great deal of nodding of heads. The audience is in agreement with the latest speaker.

Then suddenly a tall young man with an intense, serious expression steps forward. He wears a "New York Yankees" baseball cap. This young man, I am told, is Roger's brother. Obviously overwrought, he speaks with difficulty.

"I'll take the job. I'll be the assistant secretary. But only on two conditions."

The crowd holds its collective breath.

"First, that I do it only temporarily. When Roger returns he must become assistant secretary again."

The nodding heads signify assent.

"And second, if I'm going to be assistant secretary, I must get respect. The people must respect me."

This last is lost in a storm of laughter.

But Briones is not to be put off. "Any other nominations? No? Okay. All those in favor raise your hands."

A forest of arms shoots skyward.

"The matter is settled. We now have a new assistant secretary. Congratulations, compañero.*"*

Slowly, speaking softly, the Miskito people disperse. They walk, seemingly pleased, down the trail, through the night, to their homes.

———————◆———————

Peter Curwood Eubank, sixty, is a native of the Grand Caymans. He is a carpenter-fisherman. Eubank is a lean, rangy, Black man. An animated man, he smiles often, displaying a near-toothless mouth.

I came to Nicaragua eighteen years ago, and I'm a citizen of this country, though the only language I know is the one I'm using right now. Everybody around here speaks two, three languages—Miskito, Spanish, English. That's something, ain't it?

How I came to Nicaragua is something. I was working out of the Grand Caymans—that's where I'm from—on a turtle boat. The way we did turtling was that the mother ship put the crews—two or three men and a boat—off on the keys out there. We'd go turtling. Then, after a while, they'd come back and collect the men, the boat, and the turtles.

Well, they put me and my two partners off on Dead Man's Bar. Only trouble was they never did come back to collect us. We figured as how it was the end of turtling season and somehow they forgot about us. So they went back to Grand Caymans without us. Ain't that something?

So we just got in our boat and we headed downwind to the nearest land. That would be Nicaragua. That would be Puerto Cabezas. We sold our turtles right here and we kept the money and the boat.

The people told me that the fishing is good around here, and one place is the same as another, and so I just stayed on. I went fishing out there and I did pretty good. After a while I wrote to the folks back on the Grand Caymans to let them know I wasn't dead or anything like that.

After a time I married up with a Nicaraguan woman. A Miskito. A good woman. We had four kids.

Now she was from Sandy Bay. That's about thirty miles up the coast from Puerto Cabezas. There's good fishing around Sandy Bay. Good people, too. So I got me a boat and built a house in Sandy Bay. Sandy Bay is a town made up of nine villages, Miskito mostly. We lived good in Sandy Bay.

Things was going pretty good for me until this war. With the war and the contras and everything, the government says we can't go to sea anymore. Ain't that something? So what's a fisherman going to do if he can't go to sea anymore?

Well, I'm a carpenter, too. I learned to work with wood when I was a boy. That was back in the Grand Caymans. Now, there ain't no call for carpenters in Sandy Bay, but there's plenty of building going on, plenty of work, here in Puerto Cabezas.

So last January I moved here to Puerto Cabezas. My wife and four kids, they stayed on in Sandy Bay. I moved here in January. Three months later the contras raided Sandy Bay. They killed all of the soldiers in Sandy Bay, maybe twenty or thirty of them. And they killed some other people—schoolteachers, a nurse, people like that. And they killed the Miskito CDS boys and girls.

Then they took 2,200 people back up into Honduras with them. That's right—just carried them off. Now 2,200, that's near half of the people in Sandy Bay. I believe they forced most of them. But some just went along, just like that. Now, ain't that something?

My own boy, my oldest son, Pecos Allen, he's fifteen years old. Well, Pecos Allen went along with those contras, too. Did they kidnap Pecos Allen? Did he go along with them on his own? Nobody seems to know. Not even his mother. I don't even know. Ain't that something?

Those contras smashed things up something terrible in Sandy Bay. My boat, too. They smashed it in. It ain't worth nothing now. So I guess my fishing days are over. Seems that way, don't it?

All those people from Sandy Bay gone up into Honduras. I can't figure that one out.

And my boy, Pecos Allen. I'll never, never figure that one out.

———————— ◆ ————————

Two dozen men, Miskitos, are mixing cement, laying block, sawing, measuring, carrying, hammering—working on a large, barnlike building. The roof is in place. Among them is Oscar Bushy, twenty-three, a slight, young man with just a hint of a thin, wispy beard.

This building, it's a church, Seventh Day Adventist. It's a Miskito Seventh Day Adventist. That big white building there, with the brown trim, it's the English Seventh Day Adventist. The other one, smaller, with the blue, it's the Spanish church.

We had a Miskito church before. But it was wood, like the others. It was old and it got rotten, so we tore it down. This one, out of cement block, it'll last forever—or for a long time, anyway.

These men here, we're all part of the congregation. When we decided that we needed a new church we got together, and as you see, we're building it. Most everything we do outside of work is around the church.

Religion is no problem in Puerto Cabezas, in Nicaragua. We've always been totally free in our religion. Even before the Triumph. Nobody bothered us then, nobody bothers us now.

In others things yes, there have been changes. Some good, some bad. I'll tell you the bad first. The cost of everything is high and wages are low. I'm a clerk. I work for the government, in the port office. They pay me 2,000 cordobas, very little money. I couldn't be married, I couldn't have children on such a little money.

Then there are other things. My father, he's a butcher. Sometimes he used to buy a cow. He'd butcher it, and then he'd sell the meat to the stores. Now, there aren't so many cows. Also, now there are different ways, different laws. You can't buy, butcher, and sell meat in the old ways. So my father has no work. You see there are many changes. Maybe some of them are for the better, but in the meantime people who are used to the old ways are hurt.

You must be fair, though. Before the Triumph there were school fees. Now education is free. I had one year of school after the Triumph, my last year. It was free, and that was good.

Before, if you were sick you had to pay for the doctor and the medicine. Now it costs nothing. That's good.

Before, we didn't have one cement street in Puerto. Now we have some, and you can see that they're building more.

According to the government plans, things are going to get much better. I believe so, especially when this war is over. Myself, I'm not in the militia. I can't have anything to do with the military. My religion. If they call me to serve, I don't know . . . I can't. I won't handle a weapon. About that I'm certain.

I'd like to see this war over. First, because of the violence, the bloodshed. But then there are certain things that I want to do.

I don't like working in an office. I want to be a truck mechanic. Here in Puerto, the school only goes up to five years. That's okay, but not enough to learn a specialty. For that you have to go to Managua. So next year I'm going to Managua, to mechanic school.

I have two brothers in Managua. One is going to school to become an electrician. The other, he plans to go to school. Right now he has no steady work. So next year I'll be with my brothers in Managua. I'll be in truck mechanic school.

I was born here in Puerto. I like this city. I know everybody. But you know, if you want to get ahead, sometimes you have to move to other places. And that's what I want to do. I want to get ahead.

SUMOBILA

In the Miskito language Tasba Pri means "Free Land." Tasba Pri is the name of the five new asentimientos—settlements—*that have been established for Miskitos who have been forced to abandon their homes*

Sumobila

in the north along the Rio Coco. Sumobila, sixty miles west of Puerto Cabezas, is the most accessible of the asentimientos, *and it was there that I wished to visit.*

The government people were reluctant to allow me to visit Sumobila. A truck-bus had been fired upon the previous day and two Miskito women seriously wounded. (A visit to the Puerto Cabezas hospital, to the women in question, confirmed this account.) A trip to Sumobila, I was told, would require a vehicle, a driver, an interpreter, and an armed guard—all in short supply.

"Very sorry, we're concerned for your safety." "We're short of vehicles." "The road is closed." "We'll see what we can do." "Please return at ten o'clock." ". . . at twelve." ". . . at three o'clock."

At three P.M. the young Miskito woman in charge informed me that a delegation of religiosos *had arrived in Puerto Cabezas. On the following day, in a convoy, with a proper guard, they would visit Sumobila. Would I mind . . . ?*

"Of course I wouldn't mind"—particularly since I had no choice in the matter.

At seven-thirty the next morning, twenty-eight Witness for Peace delegates, in three Land Cruisers and a pickup, together with a couple of jeeps, set off along the unpaved road to Sumobila.

It was a pleasant enough trip, and the company of my countrymen and women, newly arrived in Nicaragua, was a welcome break in the sometimes grueling routine.

We passed through a vast area of young pine, a reforestation project to replace cover that had been stripped from the land during years past. The land was level, with some rolling hills. Soon we entered the forest, with occasional farms and fields. This place was poor; the land and its Miskito inhabitants on the margin. Halfway to Sumobila we crossed the heavily guarded Rio Wawa. Two Miskito boys in dugouts watched as our vehicles, in two trips, boarded the cable-ferry.

Three hours after leaving Puerto Cabezas we arrived at Sumobila, a community of 663 families—3,160 people. This place had now been the home for one, two, three years of an aboriginal people caught in the vise of a war that for the most part they didn't understand. They were the simple victims of a conflict between a new nation struggling for its survival and others cynically using these folk to regain the dominance that had been lost.

The first view of Sumobila was unimpressive. A bend in the road and there it was. No fences, no gates, simply a guardhouse on the side of the road manned (manned?) by two thirteen-year old Miskito militiamen.

The traditional stilted houses, plopped seemingly randomly along the wooded hillsides, were certainly superior to those we'd recently passed on the roadside. Every house, with an outdoor water spigot, was larger and cleaner than those in Barrio Moyé, in Puerto Cabezas. They were superior to most throughout Zelaya or, for that matter, Nicaragua.

The children seemed better dressed, equal to and more active than youngsters elsewhere in this poor land.

A visit later to the two new schools and to the health center confirmed the availability of the necessities of modern life.

The familiar pigs, chickens, and dogs wandered around and under the stilted houses. Occasional horses, burros, and cows grazed freely through the community. This was no detention facility, no concentration camp to conjure up comparisons with the Nazis. It was certainly more humane, more liveable, than the camps established for Japanese-Americans during World War II. Thick, tropical vegetation and a profusion of flowers belied any thought of punishment or "institutional" living.

Some 100 people were present in the large, cool, newly built stone Moravian church. Women, mostly, of all ages, with many children. All listened patiently, wide-eyed, as the formalities began.

I thought of the names of their villages. Waspam, Leimus, Truskatara, Bum, Sang Sang, Wiwiniak—as exotic-sounding to our ears as were these spontaneous, passionate people to our eyes.

There were speeches by the Moravian minister, the WFP delegation leader, the local Sandinista representative. I had heard the speeches before—in English, Miskito, Spanish—everything in triplicate. Necessary, of course. But formal, prepared, lacking in the spontaneity and excitement of reality.

"We greet you on behalf of our congregation. . . . Welcome in the name of God. . . . Let us come to know one another as brothers. . . . We face many difficulties today, but. . . ."

"Together, from your country and ours. . . . Sympathy and solidarity with. . . . We want to learn. . . . We wish to help. . . . Aggression. . . . Peace. . . . Brotherhood. . . . Brotherhood. . . . Peace. . . ."

All eloquent, sincere, heartfelt, and true—but speeches.

The Miskito people sat stoically, expressionless. Some of the infants squirmed in their mothers' laps. They were given the breast. Their older sisters and brothers were given leave to play in the dusty sunswept street.

The speeches wound down, flickered, and then mercifully died. The Miskito people were invited to speak.

A woman, perhaps fifty, her short hair flecked with gray, bustled to the fore. Short, stocky, barefoot, she wore a simple, flowered house dress.

"I don't want to die in the mountains. I want to die on the Rio Coco. We don't have the right food here. It's bad. In my village we had fish, rice. We had pineapple and coconut. We had everything on the Rio Coco. I don't want to die in the mountains."

Then, her fist pounding her palm, head bobbing, she repeated, word for word, her plea. "I don't want to die in the. . . ."

Finished, she looked about angrily, stamped her foot for emphasis, and returned to her place on the crowded bench.

A second woman, this one some years younger and carrying a baby, came forward, more calmly, slowly.

"We do not have the right food here. I want to see my family who has gone over to the other side. I don't want to die here. I don't want my children to be here. I want to return to my home. . . ."

A third woman, barefoot like her predecessors, entered the arena.

"I agree. I support the government. But my son was kidnapped by the contras and now he's on the other side. I understand why we had to come here. The others were going to kill us, carry us off to Honduras. But now I want my son back. We don't like this war. Every time I hear shooting I get a pain in my stomach." (There had been a major attack on Sumobila five weeks earlier, and occasional gunfire was still heard on the perimeter.)

Another woman spoke.

"In my village I had everything. Fish, oranges, bananas, beans. Everything I needed. Here I have nothing. Thank you."

A young man in his mid-twenties came forward. His shirt and trousers were work-stained, his rubber boots muddy. Short, broad, he spoke softly; his voice trembled with emotion.

"I have twenty-seven people in one house here. On the Rio Coco I had my own home. Here I have my father-in-law and his family, my brother-in-law and his family. All are under my roof. That's why I came late. I'm sorry. I just came from the forest. I'm cutting trees for a house of my own. I'm the father of two children. I need my own house. So I'm building my own house.

"Now the price of nails has gone up. I can't find a piece of zinc for a roof. I know that my house is still standing on the Rio Coco. And if it's not, I can build a new house.

"There are some here who are afraid to speak out because you'll think that they're against everything—against the government. We are not against. We only want to live as we did before. Thank you for listening to me."

A man, perhaps sixty, infirm, slowly worked his way to the front of the church.

"My five sons and my grandson were carried off by the contras. One was strangled. One was drowned in the river. I don't know where the others are. Please. Can you help to get them back for me? I'm an old man. Thank you for listening to me."

And so at Sumobila the Miskito people spoke.

We spent the night in Sumobila and in the morning awoke to the sight of children—Miskito Indians—chatting, playing, carrying their books to school. They were neatly dressed, groomed. I was struck by the fact that those who would stop the clock of history—turn it back, even—were in fact impelling its advance. Could these children ever return to the primitive, isolated, insular lives of their parents? To me it seemed highly unlikely. Amidst suffering and bloodshed a new generation of Nicaraguans was being born.

CORN ISLAND, BLUEFIELDS

The voyage south from Puerto Cabezas to Corn Island, some forty sea miles east of Bluefields, took seventeen hours. The Janet, a sixty-five-foot wooden cargo vessel, is leased and captained by Captain Howard "Harry" Simmons, a six-foot-plus, whipcord hard, one-eyed Black man of fifty-eight. The Janet plies the waters of the Atlantic coast, carrying cargo of every sort among the islands and port cities of Nicaragua's Atlantic coast.

On this 110-mile voyage the cargo is fifteen Miskito women and children—my fellow passengers—returning to their homes in Kukra Hill, a sugar-producing community near Bluefields.

Some months earlier The Janet had carried sixty or more Indians from Puerto Cabezas to Kukra Hill to labor in the sugar harvest. The harvest over, the boat had returned them to their homes together with these fifteen Kukra Hill folks who had journeyed north to visit family and friends in Puerto Cabezas. Now they—and I—are returning to Bluefields by way of Corn Island.

On Corn Island Simmons is to load coconuts for transport to Bluefields, and then inland up the Escondido River to Rama. At Rama the coconuts will be unloaded for overland transport to Managua and sale throughout the western portion of the nation.

The voyage south is uneventful save for the opportunity to come to know Harry Simmons. Like all seafaring men, Harry enjoys talk. And like all people, Harry particularly *enjoys talking about* himself.

I was an orphan. When I was very little my mommy and my daddy died. I had an older sister and she took care of me. This was all in Bluefields—that's where I was born.

But it was very hard for my sister. She did what she could for me. She looked after me, she sent me to school, but when I was nine years old I quit school and I went to work. I got jobs around the docks, around the boats. I've been a seaman ever since—I always worked around the water.

So I was nine years old and I started working around the fishing boats and shrimpers out of Bluefields. I cleaned, I scrubbed, I painted, I fixed. I worked in the galley, on deck, wherever I was needed.

Later I worked for a couple of years diving for lobster around Miskito Keys. They were all Miskito divers—and me, just one Black boy. That's where I learned to talk Miskito. I used to ask, "How do you say this?" "What do you call that?"And they'd tell me. I learned to talk Miskito pretty good. I like working with the Miskito people. They always treated me good, even when I was just a boy.

I dived for lobster for three, four years. After that I went to work on ocean-going ships. I've sailed on American, Canadian, Liberian, Panamanian, Honduran ships. I've been all over most of the world.

I always worked in the engine room. I studied, I read, I asked questions. I got a First Engineer's license. It's back home in Bluefields someplace, and I'm going to have to dig it out one of these days.

One time I sailed on deck. It was in the winter time and we went to Canada. Oh, it was cold. After that trip I went back down below and I stayed in the engine room.

I worked on shrimpers for a couple of years in the Gulf. I sailed out of Port Aranzas, Texas. That's up around Galveston. That was good work and I made good money on shrimpers.

In 1968 I came back to Nicaragua. I came home to stay. That time I got a berth on an old United States army LST. It *used to be* United

States army. Now it was converted—it was carrying cargo. I sailed as chief engineer on that LST.

After that I got a job as first engineer on a Nicaraguan tanker. The trouble with that tanker was that it was too small—you never could make any money on it.

Anyway, two years after I started sailing on that tanker she went into drydock. That was in Cartagena. Colombia. Then I decided that I wanted to do something else. I wanted to start to make some money. You see, I've got eight kids. Yes, eight kids with two women. My youngest, she's only fifteen months old now. My present woman, my wife, she's only twenty-nine.

I had my eye on this boat, *The Janet.* It used to be owned by a Chinese, by a Nicaraguan Chinese. I hear that he was against the Sandinistas, so after the Triumph they ran him out of the country.

Now the government owned this boat and it wasn't doing a thing. This is a good boat, sixty-five feet, only eleven years old. I know that this boat looks bad. That's because it hasn't been kept up. You got to keep a boat up, and in Nicaragua that's hard to do.

Like marine plywood—you just can't find it. The same with marine paint. Nails even are sometimes hard to get. Spare parts, you can't find them. And that's how a boat goes down. One thing—it has a good engine, though—a General Motors diesel. Very good engine.

I'll tell you something. I don't even have a radio on this boat. Don't even have any charts. You can't find a coastal chart in the whole country of Nicaragua. We're just sailing by guess and by golly [*laughs*].

Anyway, I made a deal with the government. They let me have the boat for so much a month. I took the boat out of the water. I scraped and painted the hull. Didn't have to do a thing with the engine, though. I sure would like to get ahold of some marine plywood, though. Those bulkheads are going.

So I got a boat and I'm in business. I carry anything for anyone. Mostly I work between Corn Island and Bluefields although I've been all up and down the coast, from Costa Rica to Honduras.

Now when we get to Corn Island, I'm going to pick up 60,000 coconuts on contract. I also bought 200 sacks for myself, to sell. Then I'll spend the night in Bluefields with my family. Next morning we'll go up the river to Rama. That's about a seven-hour trip. We'll unload the coconuts in Rama. I'll be carrying some passengers, too. Every little bit helps, right?

There's a load of steel beams for construction waiting for me in Rama—also some cement. I'm carrying the beams and some of the cement back to Bluefields. In Bluefields I've contracted to pick up some cattle, fourteen head for Corn Island. I'll carry the rest of the cement below decks, and up there in the bow, an automobile. That's right, an automobile. I told you, we'll carry anything. The car will be hard to unload in Corn Island. But I've been thinking about that. I believe we'll just lay some planks and just push her off. We'll manage—we always do.

I make a good living from this boat. But the war—you never know. Last month I was hijacked. That's right, hijacked to Costa Rica. Hijacked by counterrevolutionaries. I lost my cargo and 7,000 cordobas I had to buy some rice and beans. I almost lost my boat and my life, too.

Here's how it happened: I was carrying a mixed cargo from Bluefields to La Cruz. That's about 100 miles up the Rio Grande from Sandy Bay. It happened near Set Net point, between Pearl Lagoon Bar and the mouth of the Rio Grande.

We were just off the beach and my mate saw this turtle. It was all tangled up in a net. "Hey, dinner." So we swung around to pick up the turtle. Just as we got him on deck—"rat-tat-tat-tat." They were shooting at us from the shore and the bullets were hitting the water just in front of the boat.

On the shore there were maybe thirty, forty people in Sandinista uniforms. They signaled us to stop, and I did. I dropped the anchor. Some of them came out in a dory, five men and two women. And believe me, they were well-armed.

They came aboard—Miskitos they were. I still thought they were Sandinistas. It was the uniforms. One man said, "We want your food."

I said, "I can let you have some rice and beans, some flour, a little bit of meat—whatever we have in the galley."

He said, "What have you got below?"

"I can't touch the cargo," I said. "You know that. That cargo is government property."

He repeated his question, but this time he pointed his gun at me. Just about that time I began to suspect that these were no Sandinistas. These were counterrevolutionaries. I opened the hatch. We had a mixed cargo. We were carrying flashlight batteries, toilet paper, some clothes, soap, hardware—like that. The only food we had was a little flour and sugar.

Then they took my dory, and they started to unload. They took all of the food and some of everything else. That's when they got my 7,000 cordobas.

All day long, for seven hours, they carried my cargo ashore. They kept hauling it off into the bush somewheres. They carried off all the food and the other stuff, too.

Finally the head guy said to me, "Have you got enough fuel to go to Costa Rica?"

I said no. I really did have enough fuel to go to Costa Rica. I had plenty, but you know . . .

Then another one said, in Miskito, "Let's shoot them and burn the boat."

They didn't know that I speak Miskito. So real quick I said, "Did you say Costa Rica? I was thinking of something else. Of course. I have plenty of fuel to get to Costa Rica. More than enough. . . ."

So off we went to Costa Rica. There were seven of them and me and my crew of five. By the way, my whole crew quit me after that trip. I had to get a whole new crew. Eighteen hours later we were off Cape Limon, Costa Rica.

When we got to Cape Limon the head man said, "Would you like to stay here in Costa Rica with your crew and your boat?"

"No," said I. "I've got my family and my business in Bluefields. Besides, I'm not a Costa Rican. I'm a Nicaraguan."

He said, "You'll get some big trouble for this. You'll get ten years in jail at least."

I was so tired and mad and disgusted that I yelled at him, "Leave me alone! If I go to jail, at least it won't be a Costa Rican jail. It'll be a Nicaraguan jail."

That was just last month. I tell you, it's hard to make a living. It's getting harder all the time.

———— ♦ ————

Nicaragua's Atlantic coast faces the Caribbean. Corn Island is the Caribbean. The people are Black, Creole, Miskito. The music is Caribbean—reggae. Corn Island people earn their livelihoods from the coconut plantations, from lobstering and fishing, and from the processing plants. Their language is the vivacious patois of the islands.

The Janet was scheduled to remain on Corn Island for two or three days—and we passengers with it. So after docking I lingered as a dozen or more waterfront loafers boarded to exchange banter and the latest news with the captain and crew.

After an hour I decided to find lodging. Sam Cooper, twenty-nine, a husky Black man, suggested that as he was headed in that direction, he'd show me the way to the Islanda Hotel, about one mile down the beach. Cooper told me that he is a lobsterman:

Do you own your boat?
Yes, me and my two partners.

Is it a seagoing boat?
No. Our boat's just a big dory. We have an outboard—Japanese, a Kawasaki. It's big enough for us, except when there's weather. Then we don't go out.

How often do you go lobstering? Every day?
No. We just go out two times a week. The divers, those who go down after the lobsters, they're out five days a week. We lobster with traps.

Two days a week? Can you make a living working two days a week?
Oh yes. You see, we have 200 lobster traps. Two days a week is all we can handle. We don't own the traps. Promar does. They let us use them, and they set the schedules.

Who is Promar?
Promar, S.A. That's the lobster canning company. It's owned by the government. Before the Triumph, Promar was owned by Somoza. Before that, by Americans. Promar has always owned the lobster and fish canning factory, most of the big boats, and just about everything else on Corn Island. The small boats are owned by individual lobstermen like us.

And small lobstermen can make a living working like that?
Oh yes. In some ways much better than before. We get more help in things like health and education. We always get by. Now we get 42½ cordobas for lobster tails, which is not bad money. Our big problem is the shortages.

Shortages? Of fuel?
No. There's plenty of fuel. What we have are shortages of some kinds of food. Sometimes there's no rice. Other times we're short on milk or meat. Clothes are hard to come by. Right now I'd like to get a good strong pair of short pants. I can't find them.

Why are there shortages?
The war. When the war is over I think that it will be better. That's what they tell us. I believe it's true.

I listened to the men talking down on the dock. To tell the truth I couldn't understand their English. How do the people here feel about the government?

Some are against it. But most of the people are with the Sandinistas. You have to understand about our people here on Corn Island. They complain. They like to complain. They make jokes about the government, about the Sandinistas. They make jokes about everything. But most are with the government. They remember.

Remember what?

Before the Triumph—how it was. When Promar was owned by the Somoza people it was very different. If they didn't like you, you couldn't get traps. If you made one mistake, they'd put a lien on your boat. You couldn't joke about the government then. They had spies. They'd drive you off the island in a minute—or do worse than that. They did anything they wanted. Promar owned this island—they owned us. The people here remember. Now it's better. We can joke, we can laugh. We can talk about anything. We get respect. It's much better.

Is there any counterrevolutionary activity here?

No. There's nothing like that. Not on Corn Island.

Does your wife work?

Ophelia? No. We have three little kids and she stays home with them. She used to work in the canning factory. When the kids grow up a little, when they're in school, she'll work there again if she wants to.

How about CDS? Is there a CDS on the island?

No. But they say they're going to organize one.

What do you think about that?

That's good. I'll tell you why. Here on the island we have more than 4,000 people, and we have no hospital. We have a Centro De Salud, but we don't have a hospital and we need one. With a CDS we'll be able to organize. We'll be able to put pressure on the government for a hospital. We'll be able to organize for other things that we need, too.

When there's a CDS on Corn Island, will you join?

Oh yes. I'll join because it's for my own good—for the good of the people.

———— ◆ ————

Maria Louisa Norore Mueller is eighteen, a pretty Miskito woman.
She is active in the Moravian church.

I was born in Waspam, the largest Miskito town on the Rio Coco.
My mother and father are school teachers.

Three years ago Waspam was destroyed by the Sandinista government. They said that because of the attacks from Honduras we were
in danger of being killed. I think that they were really afraid that the
counterrevolutionaries would capture it. They were afraid that the
counterrevolutionaries would make Waspam the capital of a new
anti-Sandinista government. Could they have done this? I don't
know. I don't know anything about politics, about war.

When we were evacuated from Waspam my father went to Masaya.
He works there now as a schoolteacher. My mother is working in
Sumobila in a Miskito school. I went to Managua to continue my
education. My brothers and sisters—I have four—are in Managua
and Masaya, on the Pacific coast. You could say that the Sandinistas
detroyed my family.

I go to school and I work part-time for a Miskito lawyer. When I
finish school I don't know what I'll do. I'd like to return to Waspam,
but who knows? I don't know what the future is for me and my people.
We Miskitos, we live from day to day.

———— ♦ ————

In Bluefields a Creole in his mid-forties, said:

No, I don't have a job, and I'm not going to get one. I want only to
leave this country. I sent one son, my oldest, to stay with my friend in
Managua to avoid military service. Now I want only to take my wife
and my other son and leave this place.

These people have spoiled everything. These people don't like the
gringos. They don't want them here. They kicked them out of Nicaragua. These people refuse to see that the Americans have wealth. They
spent money. They gave us work, good jobs.

Nicaragua is a small country, a poor country. We need somebody.
The United States was like an uncle to Central America—a kind,
generous uncle to us.

———— ♦ ————

William Walker, fifty-two, is a Miskito, a carpenter. He is a broad-
faced, pleasant man who seemed pleased to interrupt his work (replac-

ing rotting slats on a wooden building) to talk with a stranger. Walker wore traditional carpenter overalls, a "Delco" baseball cap, and wire-rimmed eyeglasses.

I was born here in Bluefields. My father too. His family lived in the bush. But me, I'm a city man. Bluefields is my city. Some city, eh? [He laughs.] I raised my family here, and we're all city people.

My oldest boy, he's twenty-three, and he's in the military now. He's up along the frontier someplace. We worry about him.

My wife and I, we worry plenty. But what can we do? We didn't make the war, but we're suffering plenty. All parents with sons are suffering nowadays. But we're suffering for our children, for their children. We're suffering for the future.

———————— ♦ ————————

Alburn Downs, twenty-six, is a well-built Black man with a scrag-gly beard. He wears a bright yellow psychedelic T-shirt and well-worn dungarees.

I sell sandwiches. That's how I've been making my living lately. I walk up and down the streets of Bluefields with my big box of sandwiches. I go into the stores, into the shops. Sometimes people on the street buy them. Mostly I work around the docks, though.

In the late afternoon I buy my bread, rolls, sausage, cheese, whatever I can get. Then I make my sandwiches for the next day. I worry a lot about the food spoiling.

Sometimes I make a couple of cordobas. Some days I go broke—for instance, if I can't sell all of my sandwiches or if some of them go bad. That's when I go broke. I don't like it, but what can you do? You have to eat.

Next week I'm going to Managua to get my passport. I have an aunt in Managua, and I'll stay with her for a few days. You see, I want to get my papers so that I can get a job on a ship. I've worked on boats before, and that's the kind of work I like.

I used to work on a lobster boat here in Bluefields, the *Dipsey*. It was a Promar boat. I was the cook. *Dipsey* was a big boat—seventy-three feet. We stayed out for four weeks at a time, and you always came home with a pocket full of money. Boy, I liked that work.

We had a crew of six—the captain, the cook, and four sailors. We carried more than 500 traps. I cooked for them all, and it was fine. Good work, no worries, good money. Hey, that's the life.

The reason I'm not working there right now is that the *Dipsey* is gone. That captain was a counterrevolutionary. He and one of the men stole the boat. I think they took it to San Andreas, to Colombia. That captain, he was some Somocista. So Nicaragua lost a good boat and I lost a good job.

When I get my passport I'll go on any ship, anywhere.

Right now the future for me in Nicaragua is not good. Not for me. I think that when the war is over things will be more better. But now? For me? What can a person do?

Elections?—I don't vote. What for? It won't change anything. The only thing I want is my passport. Then I want a job on a ship.

I have a girl friend here in Bluefields. I like her very much. Maybe I'll miss her when I go. I think I will. But what can a man do? To tell you the truth, I hate the sandwich business. The only thing I want is a job on a ship—a real job.

———— ♦ ————

Nympha Delphina Taylor is twenty-nine, a Creole, She is a chambermaid-waitress at the Islanda Hotel, on Corn Island. She is a slender, hard-working, attractive women with unfailing good humor.

I was born on Corn Island, but I left as a young girl. I had an older sister who went off with a man from Managua, and she took me with her. So I grew up in Managua.

I worked at a factory in Managua where we made handbags. This factory was owned by an American, Mr. Frank Long of Tennessee. But after the Triumph Mr. Frank Long went back to America and the factory closed down.

It was very hard for me after the Triumph. I had nothing in Managua—no job. And I had two daughters. So I came back to Corn Island. Here I have a mother and a father. They helped me a little.

One of my daughters is fourteen years old, the other is eleven. I'm not yet thirty, and maybe soon I'll be a grandmother. Who knows? I had my first when I was fifteen years old.

This job is all right. I get along. But the factory was much better. There we had different machines to do different things. Here it is the same thing every day. Clean, serve, clean, serve, clean, serve. Every day the same. Today one of the girls in the kitchen is sick. So I have to do her job and mine. It's very hard.

I have a friend who works on a cruise ship in Miami, and she travels all over. It's the same kind of work as here—cleaning, washing. But on a ship it would be more interesting. I'd like to have a job like that.

Maybe someday I'll get married, but I don't think about that too much. I'd want to marry a man who'd take care of me. But maybe I'd get a man who'd want *me* to take care of *him*. Not me. Oh, no, no, no.

———————— ◆ ————————

Norman Bent, forty-seven, a Miskito Indian, is a Moravian minister.

The Sandinistas, soon after the Triumph, made many serious errors with my people. Unfortunately, they're still making mistakes with the Miskitos and other Coast people, although maybe not as much as before.

In the early days after the Triumph, with the fear of the counterrevolutionaries attacking from Honduras, they did many bad things. There were beatings, false arrests. I myself was arrested without being charged. They took me to Managua under false pretense, and they put me into solitary confinement for more than one week. They "suspected" that I was a counterrevolutionary. Later they apologized. But you don't forget these things.

Perhaps it was only natural that these things happened. These people, they know little of our history on the Coast, our culture, our way of life. Different language, different religion, different everything. They were afraid of the counterrevolutionaries. They were afraid of us. So because of fear they struck out.

Before the Triumph, the Sandinistas never administered so much as a *tienda*—a store. Now they're attempting to administer an entire nation. So how could they know about these things? They were not business managers, sociologists, statesmen. They were fighters in the mountains.

The Sandinistas want to do the right thing. They want to pull Nicaragua up from underdevelopment, from poverty, from foreign domination. I'll tell you something: Desite all of the bad things that have happened, before the Triumph I was ashamed to be a citizen of a "banana republic." Now, I'm proud to be a Nicaraguan.

5

THE WAR

The Struggle for Freedom

Today the dawn is no longer an illusion,
Tomorrow, someday, a new sun will arise
Which will shed its light on
All the land left for us by
The martyrs and heroes,
With abundant rivers of milk and honey.
  —from the "Hymn of the Sandinista Front"

The house of Concepcion Sanchez is located on a back street, a hillside alley, in the poor barrio of Danio Ponce, in Ocotal. The road before the house is unpaved, deeply rutted. Houses of mud, adobe, and weathered and scarred board are jammed one against the other. The street is crowded with children, many naked, playing in dirt amidst the dogs and chickens.

Sad-eyed women, arms folded, stand in the open doorways. They gaze without expression at the stranger, the intruder in their barrio and their lives.

This house, in its plainness, is identical to its neighbors. The door opens to a small, darkened room. The room is barren but for a cot and clippings from Barricada *and* Nuevo Diario *tacked neatly to an unpainted, scarred wall.*

A young man, fully clothed, his head buried in a tangle of bed-clothes, lies face down on a narrow cot. He remains motionless, not deigning to acknowledge the visitor.

Beyond, through an open doorway, is another room. This one is somewhat larger but equally barren of furnishings save for a crude, wooden table and four chairs. An electric light fixture hangs from the ceiling of the darkened room. There is not a curtain, picture, flower pot, radio, or any other amenity in sight.

One or two more rooms are out beyond somewhere. Perhaps one contains facilities for cooking—an oven. The other most probably has two or more cots. This home is basic, rough, poor, poor, poor. As do all in the barrio, the house has a thin zinc roof. Yet it is surprisingly cool considering the blistering heat of the day.

Concepcion Sanchez, a dark, stocky woman, smiles and nods and murmurs a word of greeting. She is forty years old, neat in a dark flowered dress. She wears no shoes.

Concepcion and Cesar Sanchez

Two young men in their mid-teens nod unsmiling greetings. A little girl, perhaps three years old, wanders through the house. From time to time Concepcion takes the child on her lap. The girl grows restless and Concepcion wordlessly sets her down. The child resumes her explorations and eventually returns to the broad, comfortable lap.

Throughout our talk tears danced in the eyes of Concepcion Sanchez. They danced, shimmered, but never quite overflowed those dark, rounded cheeks.

My son, Raul, he was killed, they tell me, on May 12. That was eighteen days ago. Raul was eighteen years old. He died in the mountains of Rio Blanca, in the Department of Matagalpa, in an ambush. There were three boys with him. Three *compañeros*. They all three died together.

A soldier came to my house. He told me. Raul lay with the others, alone, hidden in the jungle for five days. They might never have found him except for the birds, the vultures. They were flying above the bodies.

The *compañero*, he didn't tell me this, but I know—the vultures were eating his body. My boy. Some of the buzzards were flying in the sky. Others were tearing his body, eating his flesh.

I dream of this every night, every time I close my eyes. Raul, eighteen years old, and the birds tearing at his flesh.

I had three sons and one daughter. Now I have two sons. Last month my cousin's son was killed. This war is bad, bad. Sometimes I think that I'm going to lose everyone I love. All of the young men. Only God knows who will be next. My other boy, Cesar . . . *[She shakes her head sadly and nods toward the first room, toward the young man I had passed upon entering the house.]* Cesar is twenty years old, and I don't know. I don't know.

Apparently attracted by the voices, Cesar joins us. He is a slight, dark-haired young man. He wears a T-shirt, military trousers, and boots. One of the younger boys rises from his chair and Cesar sits and solemnly faces the stranger.

Nobody likes this war. We young people, we're dying, we're giving our lives every day.

I've been in the army since February, three months and two weeks. I'm home now for four days. I'm sick. They sent me home because I'm sick.

My company, we were near Wiwili. In the mountains. We walked for seventeen days, on patrol. We were searching for counterrevolutionaries. Sometimes we had nothing to eat. We found green bananas and we ate them. We drank from the streams. Sometimes we had cold rice and beans. You see, we were looking for the mercenaries. We had to be careful. We made no fires, no sounds, nothing. It was very hard, exhausting.

Finally, after seventeen days, we found them. Or maybe they found us. I don't know which. There were thirty *compañeros* in our unit. At that time we were marching to join with a much larger group.

Anyway, after seventeen days we and the mercenaries found each other. It was a very large unit. We learned later that there were 1,500 of them. We were in a valley at that moment, and they were on the heights. They had us surrounded on three sides.

Immediately, they started to shoot at us. The bullets, the shells fell on us like rain. Fortunately, the jungle was very thick. They couldn't see us. We couldn't see them. But we could hear each other clearly. We were hiding behind trees, behind rocks. The fire was so heavy that there was nothing else that we could do.

Then they called down on us to surrender. They had women with them. One of the contra women called to us to put down our weapons—to raise our arms and walk up the hill.

Nicaraguan soldiers at rest

We shouted back, "Never. We'll never surrender to a *grande puta [a great whore]*." We called her many bad names. We said we'd never surrender to any mercenary.

Then they *really* started shooting at us. They had very good equipment—very heavy stuff. It was raining steel. I'll tell you the truth. I was nervous, very nervous. A mortar shell landed near me. I think I passed out. When I recovered I felt over my whole body to see if I had been hit, if I was bleeding. Oh, I was nervous. We had no water, nothing. I was very nervous.

We couldn't move for maybe five, six hours or more. And all the while they were blasting us with rifles, bombs, mortars. They didn't let up for a minute. I was dying of thirst. I thought then that I was going to be killed.

Then we heard shooting from farther away. Ai, that was a good sound. Now *we* had the fire power. The firing was very heavy. But these were *our* mortars, *our* bombs. *We* had *them* surrounded. Our *compañeros* had arrived.

We were ordered to charge up the hill, right into the mercenaries. I was still nervous, but I ran alongside my *compañeros*. The mercenaries retreated. They ran through the jungle, and we ran after them. They couldn't regroup, and we chased them for many miles, many hours, all the time shooting, shooting. At the end of the battle we had lost sixteen *compañeros* killed. We killed twenty-three of them.

Finally, we could pursue them no longer, and we broke off the battle. I carried one of our dead on my back. I carried him for a long time, for many miles. I carried him through the mountains, down to the road. By then I was covered all over my entire body with his blood. There were many flies and other insects. He smelled, I smelled. I became sick.

They took me and others of the sick and wounded and the dead by truck to Matagalpa. I can still see this *compañero* in my mind. I can still smell his blood.

That was my first battle, and I tell you, I was nervous, very nervous. In the next battle I think—I hope—I won't be so nervous.

The mother looked toward me again.

I beg God to stop that man, that Reagan, to stop giving them guns—to stop killing our boys.

———— ♦ ————

Soldier and campesino, Jalapa

Paulo Palencia, thirty-one, works in the El Salvador Solidarity movement. Palencia has a thin, black beard. He is stocky, although not fat. He is soft-spoken, shy, almost diffident. Palencia has one hand. His left hand has been severed at the wrist.

I was born in Matagalpa to a poor family. My father was a baker. When I was a boy I, too, became a baker. Later, when I got a little older, I went to work in a small factory in Matagalpa. We made hardware—door hinges, fittings of many kinds out of brass and other metals. I liked that work much better than baking. I enjoyed working in the shop with people, with machinery.

I did clandestine work for many years. One time I had to leave Nicaragua. I was in Venezuela for two years, and I supported myself by working as a baker. So you see, my father's trade turned out to be very helpful to me.

After I returned to Nicaragua my main job was the transport of arms. In the early days I worked mostly in the north—in Matagalpa, Esteli, Ocotal. We had to be very, very careful. It was dangerous work because if the Guardia caught you they tortured you for information. Then, mercifully [*he smiles wryly*], they killed you.

In those days we transported arms in the mountains, in the forests, on trails. We used wagons, horses, and burros. We carried weapons on our backs. A gun, a box of ammunition, were jewels. An automatic rifle was worth a human life.

Later, toward the end, there was the need for great amounts of arms in Managua, Leon, and other cities. Then we had to abandon our caution. We rented cars. We drove our weapons right down the highway, past Somoza's Guardias, in rented cars.

In 1978 I was sent to Managua to participate in the August insurrection. We needed every experienced person at that time. We had many hundreds, thousands even, of devoted *compañeros* in the city. Most were young, boys and girls fourteen, fifteen, sixteen years old. They were devoted, brave beyond description, but they were untrained in the use of arms, in military tactics. We couldn't allow them to throw away their lives against the Guardias. And so experienced people were sent to Managua. The insurrection was like a school. Believe me, the young *compañeros* learned quickly.

In January 1979 I was sent to Panama. In those days there were many Chilians, Argentinians, Panamanians, Costa Ricans, and others who wanted to join with us. From Panama I went to Costa Rica to help organize and train these revolutionaries. Then we brought them into Nicaragua.

Now I think that was a mistake. Many of these revolutionaries were not ideologically strong. They were not committed to the Nicaraguan revolution or to our Sandinista leadership. Some were ultraleft—anarchists. They couldn't adapt to revolutionary discipline. Others were adventurers. They just wanted to fight—anyone. They learned nothing during the armed struggle. Some of them we had to disarm and at gunpoint put out of the country.

These people, I believe, are the base for Eden Pastora's mercenaries in the south. In the north, of course, the FDN's base are Somocista Guardias. Well [*he shrugs*], we make mistakes. And we learn.

After the Triumph I served in the army for two years. I was a political commissar. In 1981 I lost my hand and so my usefulness in the army was over. It was bad, a hard adjustment for me.

All my life, since my boyhood, I had spent doing clandestine work, in the military, studying, training, fighting—always for the revolution. All right, so that part is over.

Now I work in the Salvadoran Solidarity movement. It's important work. Necessary. After all, our struggle has no borders. The Salvadorans are our brothers, like Chilians, Palestinians, the people of South Africa—all oppressed people. It's all the same struggle—against imperialism.

I'm in the propaganda section. We make posters, pamphlets. We publish a newspaper that is distributed worldwide. Without international solidarity no revolutionary struggle can survive today against the power and ruthlessness of imperialism. Not in El Salvador, not even here in Nicaragua. And here we're strong and united. In today's world none of us could survive alone.

My main interest, of course, is here in my own country. Despite the difficulties our process is going well. Our first goal was the expropriation of Somoza's and the Somocistas' property. That has been accomplished. The land, the banks, transportation, and so much more are now the property of the people of Nicaragua.

Then there was our minimum program for health care, food, education for all of the people. This has been realized in its most basic form. We have a long road to travel, but the first steps have been taken. We are on our way.

I must admit, though, that I'm worried. I never thought that the counterrevolutionaries could strike with such force. They're doing a lot of damage. I never, not for a moment, doubt that in the end we will win. But so much suffering, so much suffering.

———— ♦ ————

There had been a contra attack in the neighborhood of Jalapa on the preceding day, so roadblocks had been established along the road. At one such roadblock on the outskirts of Jalapa all vehicles entering the town were stopped and searched. I had a brief discussion with one of six young soldiers at the roadblock.

What did you do before you were in the military?
I worked on the land.

What will you do when the war is over?
First we have to cut off Reagan's balls.

Yes, but after you've won, what will you do then?
I'll work on the land. It's what I know, what I like best. I'll get married, have many children—handsome babies, like me.

His compañeros laugh.

———————— ◆ ————————

Several miles down the road there was a second roadblock. The oldest soldier in this unit was perhaps twenty-five. He was sitting by the roadside, engrossed in a paperback book—Beirut En Llames.

Good book?
It's about Lebanon. It's the same struggle as here.

———————— ◆ ————————

Dania Buitano Colema is seventeen years old. She is the political commissar of an 800-person militia battalion. Buitano is very pretty, small, slight. Although articulate and confident, she speaks with childish reserve, shyness.

**Militiawoman, Managua,
(Dania Buitano)**

During the insurrection my brothers were doing clandestine work here in Managua. When I was ten years old one of them asked me to carry a message, an envelope, to a person in another part of the city. Of course I did it—for him. I didn't know anything about politics, about anything. I did it because my brother asked me to. I was asked to do it again and then again. That's how I became a courier for the FSLN.

I was a very little girl. I knew that it was risky and sometimes I was very frightened. I walked all through Managua. Sometimes I hitch-hiked. I took buses. I took care to keep the messages well concealed.

Most of the time I carried correspondence from the staff in charge of a cell to the combatants in the various barrios. I looked like such a baby that I was never stopped, not once, by the Guardia.

Those people, the ones who gave me the messages as well as those who received them, they talked to me. They told me about the struggle—why we were fighting, what we were fighting for. They always had time to talk to me, to explain things, to answer my questions. They gave me things to read, to study. Slowly I learned to put things together. I became a militant.

Immediately after the Triumph of the Revolution I became involved with the literacy campaign. I was still a child, but I could read, I could write. They taught me how to *teach*.

I worked in the literacy campaign in the Department of Matagalpa, in the city of Dario. I was in Dario for five months. While teaching, I myself studied. I read the works of Sandino, Fonseca, Marx, and Lenin. While I was in Dario I helped to organize the Juventud Sandinista.

Then, in 1981 and 1982 I worked in the *zafra*—in the sugar harvest. I was sent to the Julio Buitrago fields and refinery near Managua. And so you see, along with thousands of other young people, my entire life has been closely tied to our revolutionary process.

Last year the contras killed seventeen members of the Juventud in San Jose de las Mulas, in Jinotega. I was chosen to be a part of the escort to bring them home to Managua. It was an honor for me. It was also a very moving, very inspirational experience. Being near the bodies of my young *compañeros* who gave their lives for the Nicaraguan people—against counterrevolution and imperialism.

Also, last year, in October 1983, my brother Mario was a part of a unit that discovered a camp of 3,000 counterrevolutionaries near

Wiwili, in Jinotega. That small company immediately attacked the contras. Mario, along with most of the others, was killed. See our banner? Our battalion is named after my brother—The Mario Buitano Battalion.

We have 800 members in the battalion. Of course, we're all volunteers. We're men and women, boys and girls, from every kind of background. We have a seventy-two-year-old woman. She's tough, a good shot. We have one sixteen-year-old boy who is in charge of a company. I myself am only seventeen, and they gave me the responsibility of political commissar.

In the daytime I take care of my son—I have a one-year-old baby. And in the evening I go to school. Someday I want to be a journalist, a foreign correspondent. I'm now in the third year of secondary school. And when there are emergencies I drop everything and I come to headquarters.

As political commissar my job is to increase the political understanding, the moral behavior of the battalion. I have to make it clear to the *compañeros* why they do specific activities. Our militia—we fight at the frontier, we do guard duty at military, industrial, and civilian places. We do whatever is necessary, whatever we are asked to do.

For instance, next month we're going away for fifteen days of training. We're an infantry unit. Some *compañeros* will be worried about leaving their families, their jobs. We explain to them that the best way to provide security for their families is to get all of the training possible before it is too late.

Our slogan is "By training harder now you will avoid bloodshed later." We discuss this concept. We try to work collectively. But when it is necessary, we meet with individual *compañeros* and talk about it.

Being political commissar is a profound responsibility. I feel it strongly, and the *compañeros* respect my position. I have to earn that respect. By the way I behave at my work, in school, even when riding a bus, I try to earn that respect.

We all have obligations to respect one another, regardless of age or sex. It happens rarely, but I have experienced violations. That is because of my age or because I am a woman. So far I have been able to resolve this every time. Usually a political discussion is enough.

Sometimes a political discussion is not enough. Then I have my own, my personal way. I have a good temper. I've learned that when I have to I can put anyone in his right place. Anyone, anytime. Without exception. Happily, I don't have to resort to this method often.

Militiaman coffee harvester, Las Manos

The militia gives meaning to my life. Now my life projects beyond myself. I'm an important part of something really big. A historical process. To me, the militia—the struggle—is a part of history. That's like being immortal, right?

———————— ◆ ————————

Noel Palacio is twenty-two, a professional soldier. Palacio is tall for a Nicaraguan, fair-skinned, with wavy black hair. He is a serious young man, and it is only with great difficulty that one can get him to talk personally, of himself, rather than with a collective we, us, our.

I've been in the army for five years. I don't know how long I'll be in the military. I'll wear a uniform as long as I'm needed, as long as our revolutionary struggle continues.

I think that some day I'd like to work on the land. I come from a family of campesinos in Matagalpa. Whenever I return home to visit my family, I work in the fields. I enjoy that work very much.

My family was very large and very close. We had six boys and four girls. My father was in the revolutionary struggle, too, and my younger brother.

Now I'm an instructor in the military school in Managua. I work with new soldiers, mostly volunteers, young men and women. These people we're getting now, I'm very pleased with them. They come to the army with their principles well-defined.

I entered the military immediately after the Triumph of the Revolution. At that time the revolutionary process needed young men and women with strong convictions to integrate the army, to convert it from the oppressor of the people to defender and friend of the Nicaraguan people. I believe that we have succeeded in that respect.

During the years of Somoza, young people had no future in Nicaragua. We lived miserable lives, and we seemed destined to continue as our parents, as servants of the rich. The young people of my generation, though, we demanded more from life. We rebelled. The Guardias knew this, so they feared young people. They persecuted us. They killed us by the thousands.

My parents were poor campesinos. We never had anything. And so from my own experience, and with my father's example and encouragement, it was natural for me, at fifteen, to become a part of the revolutionary struggle.

I was pretty well educated for the son of a campesino—I had seven years of school. Even then, with the oppression, there was a great

The sawmill, June 3, two days after a contra attack

Maderero Yodeca, another view of June 3

Granary in Ciudad Antigua, destroyed by contras in October, 1983

Health center, Ciudad Antigua, destroyed in October, 1983

193

deal of revolutionary material available. I read of the struggles of the people of Cuba, Vietnam, Palestine, Africa, and I felt brotherhood with all of these people fighting for their freedom. I was strengthened by the knowledge that our struggle here was part of a worldwide struggle against imperialism.

When I was fifteen, sixteen I studied the writings of Sandino, Fidel, Lenin, Marx, and Engels. Sandino, of course, was my hero. All of the young people discussed his writings and the works of Lenin and Marx.

During the insurrection I was a part of the Matagalpa column. We had a strong organization with people in every town, every barrio. There were urban guerillas; there were rural guerillas who fought in the countryside and in the mountains.

Most of the time we did propaganda work. We painted slogans on walls. We passed literature. We constantly talked, talked, talked to the people. We convinced them to join us, to become a part of the

Salvaging grain at the Ocotal granary, June 3, 1984

Salvaging grain at the Ocotal granary, June 3, 1984

revolutionary struggle. The campesinos like me flocked to the Frente, especially during the latter days. The sons and daughters of the rich, though, very few of them would have anything to do with us.

We all had but two things in mind: to liberate the Department of Matagalpa and to march on Managua.

I remember just before the end, on July 18, 1979. We learned that a convoy of eighty vehicles, 2,200 Guardias, was coming to the area. They were coming from the south, from Managua. They were trying to escape to Honduras. At that time Sebaco was in the hands of the Frente. So we set up a roadblock between Sebaco and Dario. We overturned buses; we used logs, furniture. We used anything we could find to stop the trucks.

When the convoy arrived it was stopped by the roadblock, and their commander requested a meeting with us. Our leader was a young man named Justo. Justo walked forward to meet with them as they had requested. Then they opened fire and killed Justo and many other *compañeros.*

Then the battle began. We lost many men and women. Many innocent people were killed. But we won. We killed many of the fascists, and the others surrendered. Then we turned those very same vehicles around—those that hadn't been destroyed— and we marched on Managua.

It was the saddest day of my life—and the happiest. Sad for the blood that had been shed, sad for the *compañeros* who had been killed. Happy because it was the end of exploitation and injustice in Nicaragua.

EPILOGUE

Ocotal Revisited

Two days after the attack on Ocotal, on June 3, I returned to the battered city. My first stop, after finding lodging, was at Iglesia San Jose, the church. The Maryknolls were engaged in their morning prayer and devotions.

And then we toured the town. We walked amidst the carnage. The sawmill, what remained of it, was still smoldering. The coffee-processing plant and, across the road, the electric power company office were piles of debris. The building that had housed Radio Segovia was gutted; its walls pocked by gunshot and shells, as were the adjacent, residential houses.

The dead had been buried: Alberto Ruiz, Marvin Lopez, Juan Carlos Mendoza, Julio Tercero, Eusebio Quadra, along with a dozen others, most the victims of indiscriminate gunfire. Juana Maria Martinez and Maria Montalban lay in critical condition in the Ocotal hospital, along with more than fifty others, mostly women and children.

We visited the granary on the Las Manos road. Six steel silos, each with a capacity of 8,000 tons. They had been filled with corn, rice sorghum, wheat. Now they were twisted, torn, a grotesque tribute to war and destruction. In the words of the professionals, the job had been "professional."

But there was life amid the wreckage of war and counterrevolution. During the day past a call had gone out for volunteers to save the grain from the ravage of the tropical rainy season. People by the hundreds had responded. The now shattered silos had become a focal point for a demonstration of community. Graybeards, men and women, children—some barely emerged from infancy—labored to save their grain. They were poor country people for the most part, many still in shock from the events of the past forty-eight hours. One man had buried a wife two hours earlier. Wordlessly, they worked.

Some were inside the torn silos. Others stood on the cement silo platforms. They shoveled the precious grain into sacks. Others, the more fit among them, carried the sacks to waiting vehicles. Trucks of every description, jeeps, private autos, horse-drawn carts—all were pressed into service. Men pushed heavy grain-laden wheelbarrows down the highway.

The town's grain—its food—would be saved. It would be stored in municipal buildings, schools, CDS headquarters, churches—in every available shelter.

They were farmers, housewives, milita men and women, school-children, teachers, shopkeepers, laborers. Many were strangers to their neighbors-in-labor. In their labor they were brothers and sisters.

We watched this activity, awestruck. "We" were Maryknoll sisters Joan Uhlen, Rachel Pinal, and Gray Fitzgerald from Witness for Peace. Maryknoll Peggy Healy had arrived from Managua during the evening past to lend what assistance she could.

Peggy, I noted, was closely watching a band of vendors who had converged upon the site. They were hawking soft drinks, sandwiches, fruit, *nacatamale,* and other refreshments.

Peggy broke the silence of our group. "Some people might find the hawkers offensive, drawn even to tragedy. Anything to sell, to earn a few cordobas. But I don't. I find it maybe . . . even . . . somehow inspiring."

I recalled the classic *Mother Courage* by German playwright Berthold Brecht.

"Mother Courage lived and the play was set during Europe's Hundred Year War. One hundred years of war. Death, plague, devastation, brutality, pestilence. Hell on earth.

"Mother Courage earned her bread by selling. She was a vendor, a peddler. She pulled a cart, and from this cart she sold her products— sometimes hardware, sometimes dry goods, food, clothing. Anything. Everything. She dodged bullets and bombs. She lived amidst death and disease. She lost her two sons—all that was dear to her. But Mother Courage never lost heart. She survived through sheer will. She never, despite the agony of her existence, faltered.

"This play, *Mother Courage,* is a tribute to the human will and capacity to survive. That's what we're witnessing here today. These people will survive."

"And," someone added, "they will prevail."